What people are saying about …

SIFTED

"What a hot shower is to coal mining, Rick Lawrence's book *Sifted* is to the 'dirty secrets' of discipleship. The question 'why do bad things happen to good people?' or 'why do good things happen to bad people?' is answered here differently than you'll find in any other place: by an invitation to journey with Jesus into the cribs, caves, and coal mines of human existence."

Leonard Sweet, best-selling author, chief contributor to Sermons.com, and professor at Drew University and George Fox University

"The book you hold in your hands is spiritual dynamite! *Sifted* is going to blow your world up! And then God is going to lovingly, carefully, and—like the Master Builder He is—skillfully rebuild you into a deeper, thicker, better Christlike and Christ-infused you. This is one of the best books I've ever read."

Derwin L. Gray, lead pastor of Transformation Church and author of *Hero: Unleashing God's Power in a Man's Heart*

"It is not very helpful to talk about pain in a depersonalized, ideological way. What Rick has done, instead, is to give us a deeply personal book where conversations about suffering and faith and evil and a loving God are anchored in the story of Scripture and embedded in the stories of his life and the lives of his friends. Trials and testing are not abstractions in these pages; they are as vivid and textured as they are in our own lives. And because of that, the hope that we find in these pages is just as real."

Glenn Packiam, executive pastor of spiritual formation and lead pastor of New Life Sunday Night at New Life Church, and author of *Butterfly in Brazil, Secondhand Jesus,* and *Lucky*

"I've been an avid fan and follower of Rick's work for years. He has a heart for Jesus, a passion for people, and a way with words that penetrates the soul. Rick is a thinker, a teacher, and a motivator, and I'm thrilled that another Rick Lawrence book is in print!"

Doug Fields, speaker and author of *Fresh Start, Refuel,* and *What Matters Most,* www.dougfields.com

"Have you ever read a book cover to cover only to have the content become a major part of your thinking even after you are finished? I loved this book, and that's exactly what happened with me when I read *Sifted.* Not only do I respect and admire Rick Lawrence, but his message in *Sifted* can change the way you look at life. This is an extraordinary book, and I have no doubt you will draw closer to God as you read it. Don't miss the opportunity for a life-changing experience as your heart is warmed with hope and guidance."

Jim Burns, PhD, president of HomeWord and author of *Teenology, The Purity Code,* and *Confident Parenting*

sifted

GOD'S SCANDALOUS RESPONSE TO SATAN'S OUTRAGEOUS DEMAND

RICK LAWRENCE

David C Cook®

transforming lives together

SIFTED
Published by David C Cook
4050 Lee Vance View
Colorado Springs, CO 80918 U.S.A.

David C Cook Distribution Canada
55 Woodslee Avenue, Paris, Ontario, Canada N3L 3E5

David C Cook U.K., Kingsway Communications
Eastbourne, East Sussex BN23 6NT, England

LCCN 2011929503
ISBN 978-1-4347-0074-2
eISBN 978-1-4347-0448-1

Published in association with the literary agency of WordServe Literary
Group, Ltd., 10152 S. Knoll Circle, Highlands Ranch, CO 80130.

The Team: Terry Behimer, John Blase, Amy Kiechlin
Konyndyk, Sarah Schultz, Caitlyn York, Karen Athen
Cover Design: Brand Innovation Group
Cover Image: iStockphoto, #8881373

Printed in the United States of America
First Edition 2011

1 2 3 4 5 6 7 8 9 10

053011

TO MY "TRUE FAMILY" AT GREENWOOD COMMUNITY
CHURCH IN DENVER, FOR BLOWING ON MY
EMBERS AND FIRING MY PASSION FOR FOLLOWING
THE "BEELINE TO JESUS" IN ALL THINGS.

CONTENTS

ACKNOWLEDGMENTS

Thank you, Beverly Rose, for first suggesting this labor of love to me, then prodding me to do it, then hounding me to do it—I could never have written this work without your support and belief in me. And I would never be the man I am without the fierceness of your love; your ability to be simultaneously impressed and unimpressed with me is my own personal sluice box. A beautiful sluice box.

Thank you, Lucy Rose and Emma Grace, for launching yourselves into my arms whenever I return from being away, for loving me for who I am in your life, not for what I do, and for wallpapering my office at home with handmade treasures and reminders of your beauty.

Thank you, Tom Melton, for spoiling me with an overabundance of your invigorating presence—offering your "good treasure" with extravagant generosity and giving me a kindred spirit as a companion on this grand adventure. And thanks for calling me "Nancy Drew" when, of course, "The Hardy Boys" was an available option.

Thank you, Bob-Stud Krulish, for the five thousand ways you've poured your life and wisdom into me—your spirit "hovers over" these pages.

Thank you to those who read this manuscript in advance and offered both your encouragement and your critique: Kathy Dieterich, Linda Droeger, Sherrie Farrell, Jill Guerrero, Bob Krulish, Jill Melton, Tom Melton, and John Queen.

Thank you to John Queen for standing in line for hours in the early-morning freeze, waiting with me to get a KBCO Studio C CD, and responding to my doubts about this book with matter-of-fact belief in me—that was a real turning point for me.

Thank you to all those who so generously gave me the space and real estate to write this labor of love: The monks of St. Benedict's Monastery, Gary and Jeanne Hague, Gary and Deb Oberg, Rick and Mary Jo Krump, the Carter Morrison family, and the Mount St. Francis Retreat Center.

Thank you to all the artists who formed the backdrop for this work—I'm profoundly indebted to you: Alison Krauss, Andrew Osenga, Andrew Peterson, the Avett Brothers, Barenaked Ladies, the Beatles, the Blackthorn Project, Bob Dylan, Brad Corrigan, Bruce Cockburn, Chet Baker, Counting Crows, David Rawlings, Diana Krall, Dispatch, Ella Fitzgerald, Elvis Costello, Frank Sinatra, the Fray, Gillian Welch, Glenn Packiam, Gungor, the Hold Steady, Indigo Girls, Iron & Wine, Jakob Dylan, Jars of Clay, Joe Henry, Johnny Cash, Jonatha Brooke, Josh Ritter, the Low Anthem, Lucinda Williams, Lyle Lovett, Marc Cohn, Mark Knopfler, Mavis Staples, Miles Davis, Mindy Smith, My Morning Jacket, Natalie Merchant, the Normals, Patty Griffin (!), Pearl Jam, Peggy Lee, Peter Wolf, Robert Plant, Ramsey Lewis Trio, Rickie Lee Jones, Robert Randolph and the Family Band, the Rolling Stones, Rosanne Cash, Rosie Thomas, Ryan Adams, Sara Groves, Sarah McLachlan, Sheryl Crow, Sondre Lerche, Spoon, Steve Winwood, Steven Curtis Chapman, Sting, Sufjan Stevens, Toad the Wet Sprocket, Tom Waits, Tonio K. (!), U2, Vampire Weekend, Van Morrison, Vince Guaraldi, and Wilco.

And, finally, thank you, Greg Johnson at WordServe Literary, for your wise and valuable advocacy. Thank you, Terry Behimer and Don Pape of David C Cook, for going "all-in" with me. Thank you, Caitlyn York, for your bulldoggery (I know, not a real word) as you copyedited this book. And, especially, thank you, John Blase at Cook, for your friendship—and for your passion, skill, and surgical restraint. You've all had the faith of my own personal "cloud of witnesses" and the MO of a "good shepherd" in my life.

INTRODUCTION

"Show me a hero and I'll show you a tragedy."
—F. Scott Fitzgerald

For my birthday one year my wife gave me a book about Sir Ernest Shackleton, the legendary explorer who in 1914 attempted to be the first to circumnavigate Antarctica from sea to sea, only to endure epic hardships after his ship (prophetically named the *Endurance*) got stuck in pack ice.[1] For most of the ensuing year the *Endurance* slowly morphed from a seagoing icebreaker to a ghostly frozen outpost, with its rigging sheathed in ice and its desperate crew counting on the spring thaw to set them free again. But instead the thaw sent hulking blocks of bluish ice crashing into the ship's thick hull. And after a month spent bracing themselves against the pummeling, the twenty-seven men of the *Endurance* abandoned ship, camping on the pack ice as the sea's frozen incisors slowly chewed and swallowed its timbers. The last to slip below the surface was the mast, a barren tree on the frozen expanse. And in the eerie aftermath Shackleton's men knew that catastrophe was about to accelerate into tragedy. They were almost a thousand miles from help, with dwindling provisions, subzero weather, no means of communication, grinding ice behind them, and treacherous waters in front of them. And no *Endurance*.

One thing they had going for them—some historians would say the *only* thing they had going for them—was the remarkable will of Ernest Shackleton, a man whose capacity for hope seems borrowed from heroic fiction. By the following summer he had *willed* the entire party—every last man who'd been on that ship—safely home. They had to eat their beloved sled dogs to survive. They had to fit up salvaged lifeboats for a harrowing five-day journey over open water to the temporary safety of Elephant Island. They had to fashion a makeshift sail for Shackleton and five of his men, then point the largest of their lifeboats toward a distant whaling station on South Georgia Island, across the widow-making Southern Ocean. Along the way they had to survive twenty-foot swells that often engulfed their twenty-two-foot boat, a kind of sleepless dementia that reduced some of the men to a catatonic fetal position, frostbitten fingers encased in ice and frozen to the oars, and navigational challenges akin to sinking a basket from the upper deck (historians call it the single greatest feat of open-boat navigating ever). Once the men were in sight of South Georgia's craggy shores, hurricane-force winds threatened to smash the boat on outlying rock formations. Finally, the half-dead men hauled their little boat onto the shore of a tiny rock cove. And then Shackleton and two of his men had to cross the width of the island's forbidding, unmapped, mountainous interior in one thirty-six-hour all-or-nothing death march to the whaling station on the leeward side of the island.

The men, determined apparitions, stumbled out of the frozen mist of the mountains and shuffled into the Stromness station, where the shocked workers at first insisted their story couldn't be true. From that moment, Shackleton's name was legend.

Apsley Cherry-Garrar, writing about his experiences with the great Antarctic explorer Robert Scott in his book, *The Worst Journey in the World*, says: "For a joint scientific and geographical piece of organization, give me Scott; for a Winter Journey, Wilson; for a dash to the Pole and nothing else, Amundsen: and if I am in the devil of a hole and want to get out of it, give me Shackleton every time."[2]

Now, that's some kind of a man.

It's an understatement to say Shackleton's story captured me— the effect was more like addiction. I took the book with me on a four-day vacation, and every morning I'd get up at 5:00 or 6:00 a.m. and eat through its pages like a starving man. Shackleton's courage romanced me—his capacity for swallowing pain and then persevering mesmerized me. It was hard to resist the lure to worship him as if he were a kind of god.

But the final scenes in Shackleton's life are unbearably and heart-breakingly human.

Away from the heroic challenges of his Antarctic explorations, he was ill equipped for the normal life of a husband and father. He grew restless for the financial security that had eluded him all his life, so he launched many wrongheaded and failed business ventures, ultimately descending into alcoholism and dying of a heart attack more than $1 million in debt.

The story's end bashes hard against the soul.

How is it possible that the same kind of everyday frustrations and failures common to you and me should cut the legs out from under a man of this magnitude? How could he survive the harshest conditions on earth but crumple under the weight of his mortgage?

The thought of a transcendent figure like Shackleton disintegrating because of the assaults of his day-to-day disillusionments fueled a kind of outrage in me. I turned the last page then snapped the book shut to punctuate my frustration and dissonance. If the drip-drip-drip of our everyday pains, those familiar discouragements and imploded hopes, can eat away the soul of a giant, then what chance do we relative midgets have? Titanic resolve compressed Shackleton's soul into granite; then a thousand tiny pains consumed it, like rock-eating termites.

Later that year I read about a similar dismantling at work in the story of Meriwether Lewis, the incomparable leader of the greatest expedition in North American history.[3] He, like Shackleton, led a handpicked group of brave men in one of the most improbable feats of survival ever recorded, returning from his explorations of the western frontier with every last man (save for one who died of an unknown illness) safely home. But forced to merge back into the flow of normal life, Lewis tried and failed to handle its challenges, slowly disintegrating into a shell of his former self and ultimately committing suicide.

In my soul something dark and dreadful grows. How am I to beat back the rock-eating termites when they swarm? In *A Long Obedience in the Same Direction* Eugene Peterson writes: "Unpleasant things happen to us. We lose what we think we cannot live without. Pain comes to those we love, and we conclude that there is no justice. Why does God permit this? Anxiety seeps into our hearts. We have the precarious feeling of living under a Damoclean sword. When will the ax fall on me? If such a terrible thing could happen to my friend who is good, how long until I get mine?"[4]

The Damoclean sword ("the threat of imminent harm") that is Shackleton's story reminds me that it's so often *not* the big things that bring us down; even we midgets somehow summon the courage to face obvious life-threatening challenges. Rather, it's the everyday holocausts that carry the leverage to take us out—the sucker punches that buffet us when all we're trying to do is raise our kids, work our jobs, and make sure we have perpetual access to a good four-dollar cup of coffee.

The Attack of the Termites

In an email response to a close friend who'd written to encourage us, my wife chronicled our own infestation of termites after a church leader blindsided us with a painful accusation, leaving us feeling pummeled and crushed:

> Life has simply been overwhelming for me. I received your emails after a very trying and exhausting time. I haven't had the energy to respond. Your words were nourishing for my soul. Actually, it was hard to really take them in. I wanted to dismiss them in light of what recently happened to Rick and me. On top of [the accusation], in the last ten days:
>
> • Both of our cars have needed expensive repairs—Rick's just suddenly stopped on the street and could have led to a catastrophic accident if it had been on

the highway where he does most of his driving.

- We have mounting financial pressures from my extraordinary medical care, and we're scrambling to find ways to address them.

- Emma broke two bones in her wrist the night before we were to leave for Seattle for a friend's wedding—we spent the night in the emergency room with her, wondering if we should simply cancel the trip.

- A copper water pipe broke in our crawl space, pouring water into our basement area an hour before we were to leave for the airport.

- I reached a tipping point in my parenting challenges, and we went to meet with a family therapist this week to deal with our issues.

- Our garage door broke, leaving us stranded in our house an hour before Rick was to go and teach a new class at church.

- I started on an antidepressant drug because things just became too overwhelming for me.

No, there are no capital-T tragedies on this list—they are simply the vanguard of the army of rock-eating termites. And, as you might suspect from your own termite infestations, a little over a month after my wife wrote this note we'd already fumigated most of them....

- We'd met face-to-face with the person who'd accused us and had started down the path toward reconciliation.
- We'd somehow found a way to fix both cars.
- We'd refinanced our house to put ourselves in a better financial situation.
- My six-year-old daughter, Emma, was out of her cast and somersaulting around the house again.
- We'd met twice with a family counselor, and our home environment was much more peaceful and kind.
- A plumber fixed our water pipe while we were away in Seattle.
- The garage door is as good as new.
- The mild antidepressant Bev took helped stabilize a downward spiral of emotions.

No one died. No one was abducted by aliens or Richard Simmons. No one gave up or gave in. But for a long while we wondered how much we could handle before the walls crumbled around us, as Aragorn and his warrior companions must have felt defending the gates of Helm's Deep in *The Two Towers*. So we survived the swarm … again. And the wizard Gandalf thunders down the mountain with his army of horsemen to save the fighters at Helm's Deep—a day-late rescue that smells a lot like most of our own rescues.[5] But what's

left of our ramparts after the assault? Smashed walls. The dead. The
traumatized survivors. I've always heard that "whatever doesn't kill
you makes you stronger"—well, it might also be true that "whatever
doesn't kill you maims you." We walk with limps, but we hide them
well behind our stiff upper lips.

Max Lucado writes: "Many live their lives in the shadows.
Many never return. Some dismiss…. 'Well, everybody has a little
slip now and then.' Some deny…. 'These aren't bruises. These
aren't cuts. I'm as healthy as I've ever been. Me and Jesus? We are
tight.' Some distort…. 'I'm not to blame. It's his fault. It's society's
responsibility…. Don't point the finger at me.' When we fall, we
can dismiss it. We can deny it. We can distort it. Or we can deal
with it."[6]

We know this truth about following Christ: Pain abounds, but
grace abounds more. But is this alchemy mutually dependent? Has
God decreed that we gorge on one to taste the other? And why is it
such a *certainty* that pain abounds?

One of my favorite songs is Tonio K.'s "You Will Go Free"—the
first stanza perfectly sums up what C. S. Lewis called "the problem
of pain":

> *You've been a prisoner …*
> *Been a prisoner all your life*
> *Held captive in an alien world*
> *Where they hold your need for love to your throat like a knife*
> *And they make you jump*
> *And they make you do tricks*
> *They take what started off such an innocent heart*

And they break it and break it and break it
Until it almost can't be fixed[7]

Pain breaks and breaks and breaks. It's as if we stumbled into the middle of the gods at batting practice, our heads repeatedly mistaken for the ball. And in the devastated emotional landscape that remains after our breaking, these questions sit in the rubble:

- "Who are the 'they' that are 'breaking and breaking and breaking' my heart?"
- "Why are 'they' doing this to me?"
- "Why does God feel like such a fickle ally—if He's supposed to be for me, why does it so often seem that He's against me?"
- "Where can I find relief, and what will it cost me to get it?"
- "What can I do to stop this from happening again, and who will show me the secret formula?"
- "How will I go on, now that I know this can and will happen to me?"

Our False GPS

Our questions about the pummeling we experience seem scandalous—we know we're not supposed to ask them out loud in polite company. Our job is to be good soldiers, keeping our noses to life's grindstone even when God seems terribly unconcerned about the rock-eating termites chewing away at us. So we stumble our way around in the dark, trusting a kind of false GPS for our souls—the fundamental belief that the universe rewards good people with a good life and punishes bad people with their just deserts. When bad things happen to good people our first reaction is disbelief and amazement—it's a sucker punch—because "it doesn't make sense." Right? Our GPS is no help here. And even though we wouldn't phrase it just this way, we treat the universe of non-good people as if it were as tiny as a mustard seed—Hitler, for sure, and Saddam Hussein and Osama bin Laden and Pol Pot and child sexual abusers and the DMV in general. But pretty much all the people we know consider themselves "good" and therefore fundamentally undeserving of the beating they're taking from the pain actually meant for the tiny secret society of "bad people."

Peterson writes:

> We have been told the lie ever since we can remember: human beings are basically nice and good. Everyone is born equal and innocent and self-sufficient. The world is a pleasant, harmless place. We are born free. If we are in chains now, it is someone's fault, and we can correct it with just a little more intelligence or effort or time.
>
> How we can keep on believing this after so many centuries of evidence to the contrary is difficult to comprehend, but nothing we do and nothing anyone else does to us seems to disenchant us from the spell of the lie. We keep expecting things to get better somehow. And when they

don't, we whine like spoiled children who don't
get their way.[8]

Several years ago I surveyed almost ten thousand Christian teenagers and adults serving together in a summer outreach program and
asked them this question: "Can a good person earn eternal salvation
through good deeds?"[9] One out of five Christian adults answered
yes, and twice that percentage of teenagers agreed. And, I have to say,
I think these were just the honest ones. After decades spent asking
Christian people questions like this one and comparing their answers
to how they—and I—actually live, I'm positive that most of those
who answered with the theologically correct no are functionally living their lives in contradiction to their beliefs. I mean, we say it's
God's goodness, not ours, that saves us. But you'll understand your
own "functional theology" when you realize how quickly you get
defensive when someone hints that all is not "well with your soul" or
how quickly you think ill of someone who's going through repeated
hardships.

As an elder at my church I'm on the list to receive a weekly
report of all the prayer requests that have been formally submitted to
us. I've noticed that there are a handful of people who always show
up on the list, and I've also noticed that I must fight the temptation to agree with a subtle-but-brazen judgment that whispers in my
head: "That person must be messed up." Can you relate? If you can,
we're both in the company of Job's friends, who were pretty sure the
great man was hiding his festering sins under a legendary veneer of
goodness. And they were even more sure that God had pointed a
sewer pipe of catastrophic circumstances at their friend and opened

wide the valve, essentially blasting away at him with the brown stuff until he admitted what *had to be true*—that he deserved what he was getting. In the functional theology of Job's friends—and, as it turns out, our own—God is well qualified to work as an interrogator at Guantanamo Bay or Abu Ghraib. He will surface what we're hiding by torturing it out of us....

This is exactly why the book of Job is known by most but studied by few—its premise frightens and confuses us. Good thing the outcome is a fairy-tale ending, or the whole thing would be unendurable—an even less likely choice for the midweek women's Bible study. Job's friends, later discredited and lambasted by God, believe exactly what we believe: that no matter what we tell ourselves to the contrary, good people are rewarded in life and bad people are punished. The certainty of this equation means that Job, because of his kitchen sink full of tragedies, must assuredly be hiding some secret (and whopper) sins. His friends' approach to counseling makes logical sense—reveal what you've done wrong, repent of it, and maybe God will turn off the spigot.

So some of us, following the advice of Job's friends, respond by repeatedly begging for God's blanket forgiveness for the vaguest of sins or by finding someone or something to blame for our catastrophes. Many more of us respond by determining to work ever harder to be good, or by keeping our bad carefully camouflaged, or by vowing to trudge on under an ever-increasing burden of doubt and guilt—or by metaphorically jabbing our finger at God and threatening to outwit and outlast Him, as if we were the last two competitors on *Survivor*. In the seasons of our lives when we feel as if we can relate to Job, we often struggle with shame. It's the shame of our failure to measure up to God's exacting standards of goodness, the same unreasonable shame that Job's friends "gifted" their friend with.

We Still Haven't Found What We're Looking For

One Saturday afternoon, I was running errands in my car and listening to National Public Radio's award-winning show *This American Life*. Host Ira Glass is the medium for the life stories of average people who've experienced extraordinary moments. On this day, I was captured by the story of a young woman, Trisha Sebastian, whose best friend had died suddenly from an aggressive cancer. She told Glass that her friend was "such a good person," and, therefore, her death was all the more a tragedy. Why, she asked, would God allow "someone like me to still be here when someone like Kelly … who spread so much good throughout the world, in her own little way … it just doesn't make sense." This was the reason, she told Glass, that she no longer believed in God. Soon after her friend's death, Sebastian decided on a whim to contact a Christian football coach who'd been in the news recently. The coach had encouraged his school's fans to root for their opponent, a team made up of kids from a juvenile detention center. Sebastian was looking for answers about her friend's death, for a pathway back to God, and she admired what this man had done. "I'd been struggling with this grief that I feel over my friend's death, and I thought that he would be able to counsel me and console me," she told Glass. "And what happened instead was that he basically brought out argument after argument, like, saying that the theory of evolution is contradicted by a seventh-grader's textbook, and—" Glass broke in to say, "Oh, I see—he was trying to argue with you about the existence of God instead of trying to comfort you." Sebastian responded, "Yeah,

I think that was it…. And that completely turned me off towards him. And now I'm left with all of these questions…. Deep down, I really want to believe again." So Glass suggested she call the coach again, with him on the line, so that her real questions about her friend's death could be addressed.

But instead of directly focusing on her fears and confusion, the coach tried to explain the ramifications of original sin to her. And that left the desperate, grieving woman full of angst and unanswered questions. I listened to the whole interchange and could feel my own tension mount as the coach tried to answer this disconsolate woman with an earnest lesson in apologetics. When she asked the coach to, instead, help her understand a God who would do this kind of thing, he responded: "This is the most common question that folks who are anti-God ask—this is the most common objection to God. Why does God allow bad things to happen to good people? You have to understand that sin entered the world through one person: Adam. Now, if you read what the Bible says happened as a result of sin, every single person who's ever been born was born into sin—" And at this point Sebastian interrupted him with this: "So, I'm sorry to break in, but you're saying cancer is caused by sin?"

As earnest and good-hearted as the coach was, his explanations did nothing to bring peace to Sebastian's soul. We, like her, just don't understand the basic unfairness of pain. Even though we've prayed and read books and listened to sermons and talked to wise friends, we agree with Bono's wail—"I still haven't found what I'm looking for."

Ultimately, the "Why this pain?" question haunts us because we're profoundly unsatisfied with the answers we get. I'm inexorably drawn to Shackleton's story at the same time I'm haunted by it, like a moth circling a bug light at night. It's a mystery, and the solutions our theological Sherlocks offer us don't seem to solve it for us. They explain it, it makes sense, and it does nothing to calm our souls. That's because the Job story hints at something that is *simply unacceptable*—that not only does God Himself not intervene in all of our tragedies, He's actually a *coconspirator* in some of them. If our good God, like a double agent, can unpredictably join in the destructive schemes of our enemy, "how great is the darkness" (Matt. 6:23)? In the wake of his twenty-five-year-old son's death in a climbing accident, philosopher and Yale University professor Nicholas Wolterstorff wrote:

> I believe in God the Father Almighty, maker of heaven and earth and resurrecter of Jesus Christ. I also believe that my son's life was cut off in its prime. I cannot fit these pieces together. I am at a loss. I have read the theodices produced to justify the ways of God to man. I find them unconvincing. To the most agonized question I have ever asked I do not know the answer. I do not know why God would watch him fall. I do not know why God would watch me wounded. I cannot even guess.[11]

These are *not* entertaining mysteries—they are mysteries that wound and pummel and empty us. We can't help ourselves; we're driven to extremes just as King David was in the Psalms: "Why do You stand afar off, O Lord? Why do You hide Yourself in times of trouble?" (Ps. 10:1). This is why the conspiracy embedded in Job's story is so unnerving to us, and it would be even more so if it wasn't relegated to the Old Testament where, we tell ourselves, the stories seem so distant and over the top that they're really more like moralistic fairy tales than actual accounts of actual people and their actual dealings with God. So we put stories like this *not* on the back burner of our lives but hidden under the stove where we don't have to *really* look at them … ever.

But these stories, like cockroaches, keep creeping out from under the stove—especially at night, when the lights go out. We're reading along in the comfortable environment of the Jesus-loves-me New Testament and we ram right into a story about Him that, finally, makes it nearly impossible to avoid the scary truth. It happens at the end of the Last Supper, right before Jesus is betrayed, stripped, scourged, paraded through the streets, and nailed to a cross:

> In the same way, after the supper he took the cup, saying, "This cup is the new covenant in my blood, which is poured out for you. But the hand of him who is going to betray me is with mine on the table. The Son of Man will go as it has been decreed, but woe to that man who betrays him." They began to question among themselves which of them it might be who would do this.
>
> Also a dispute arose among them as to which of them was considered to be greatest. Jesus said to them, "The kings of the Gentiles lord it over them; and those who exercise authority over them call themselves Benefactors. But you are not to be like that. Instead, the greatest among you should

be like the youngest, and the one who rules like the one who serves. For who is greater, the one who is at the table or the one who serves? Is it not the one who is at the table? But I am among you as one who serves. You are those who have stood by me in my trials. And I confer on you a kingdom, just as my Father conferred one on me, so that you may eat and drink at my table in my kingdom and sit on thrones, judging the twelve tribes of Israel.

"Simon, Simon, Satan has asked to sift you as wheat. But I have prayed for you, Simon, that your faith may not fail. And when you have turned back, strengthen your brothers."

But he replied, "Lord, I am ready to go with you to prison and to death."

Jesus answered, "I tell you, Peter, before the rooster crows today, you will deny three times that you know me." (Luke 22:20–34 NIV)

Here we are at the Last Supper, with the cross shading every interaction, and Jesus turns to Peter and reveals something that's most certainly happening behind the scenes, right then at history's cross-roads. He confides in Peter, like a friend who whispers in your ear what the neighbors *really* think of you, that Satan has asked to "sift [him] like wheat." And, even more disturbing than this revelation, Jesus doesn't reassure Peter that He will *not allow* this terrible thing to happen—instead, He tells him that He has prayed that his "faith may not fail" and "when you have turned back, [that you would] strengthen your brothers." This "sifting" is going to happen, it's going to happen with Jesus' permission, and it's going to happen for a reason.

You Will Go Free

Is it possible that God is a coconspirator in our own stories of sifting?

And if so, *what is He really after in us?*

And however I answer this question, can *anything* be worth the price of the pain I've experienced, or will soon?

In this story—in these three sentences uttered by Jesus to Peter—He pulls back the curtain on what's happening, all the time, in an unseen spiritual world where the forces of darkness demand entrée into our lives. He also bares His goodness. I know this makes no sense on the face of it—our realities are too cruel and the pain too central for the shallow and offensive formulas that are pandered to us. But this is no formula—it's a journey into the deeper recesses of the heart of God, a path well stumbled by the saints of God throughout history and in the lives of those who've had the biggest impact for good in our own lives.

All of the people and books and music and films you and I love the most are encrusted, like priceless jewels, with pain. Name something that captures your heart that was not formed by pain. It's ironic, of course, that pain repels us more fundamentally than anything else in life but it produces things that are magnetic to us. Why do we live in fear of pain while, at the same time, we find ourselves drawn to its "produce" in the people and stories of our lives? And why does all great art, and why do all truly great people, seem positively marinated in pain?

The mystery of our sifting is a trek into the kind of raw intimacy God once shared with His beloved Adam and Eve—it is the brutal outworking of redemption, hope, and joy in our lives. But the journey is no stroll—it's an epic and terrible adventure. A treasure hunt.

And that treasure is our freedom.

Paul reminds us of the fundamentals: "It is for freedom that Christ has set us free" (Gal. 5:1 NIV). And, it turns out, the "epic and terrible adventure" that is the story of our journey from bondage to freedom is fraught with danger and heartbreak. Danger is an essential aspect of any adventure; without danger, it's not really an adventure. Stopping to buy a cup of coffee does not qualify as an adventure, but it might if you're in Baghdad. Landing an airplane on a runway is usually no adventure, but it is if your runway is the Hudson River. The danger we must face down in our own adventures is the threat of the rock-eating termites—it's the pain that eats away at us and the terrible offense of our sifting. But the point of our lives is *not* the pain—we are not pawns of a capricious deity or the collateral damage of an ancient metaphysical feud. We are prisoners—freedom is our only hope and sifting is its currency.

While the first stanza in Tonio K.'s song "You Will Go Free" describes the "breaking and breaking and breaking" we experience in life, his refrain is the counterpoint—it exactly describes the promise that carries us through the tunnel of our darkness:

> *Well, I don't know when*
> *And I don't know how*
> *I don't know how long it's gonna take*
> *I don't know how hard it will be*
> *But I know*
> *You will go free*[12]

JUST A LITTLE NIGHT MUSIC

(A Kind of Preamble)

> We would very soon become contemptuous of a god whom
> we could figure out like a puzzle or learn to use like a
> tool. No, if God is worth our attention at all, he must be
> a God we can look up to—a God we *must* look up to.
>
> —Eugene Peterson, *A Long Obedience in the Same Direction*

To Peter, and to us, the revelation that Satan has asked to sift him and that Jesus has given His permission is a lightning strike. What happens here, in the seven sentence fragments that make up Jesus' compact revelation, is a tipping point in history. Luke 22, where this revelation is embedded, may be *the* epic chapter in the entire Bible. "The Seven Sentence Fragments That Changed the World" come at the end of this chapter, after an impressive stampede of events artificially corralled by the boundaries hammered out by the Council of Nicaea in AD 325.[1] The context for Jesus' words is so crucial for us to understand; because God is telling us a story that will save us, we risk everything when we simply extract these tipping-point fragments from their context.

Context, whenever we're considering the Word of God, is more accurately labeled "narrative." It is not the linear march of numerals in an equation; it is the pounding of a heart. This is what separates the novelist from the microbiologist and the poet from the physicist and the singer/songwriter from a guy breaking up a sidewalk with a jackhammer—context to the first is vital to the truth in the same way that melody is vital to the lyrics of a good song; context to the second is simply a technical consideration.

So, before we can go further, we *must* jump-start the rhythm of the narrative in our soul—*the vitality of the context*—by first taking a quick plunge into the muddy-deep verses of Luke 22:1–19....

Scene 1: Judas secretly meets with the chief priests and scribes to hammer out the details of his betrayal.

More than once, the conspiratorial Jewish leaders, bound by an assassin's pact, have plotted to take out Jesus, failing each time (Matt. 26). These are men used to getting their own way—proficient, as Jesus charged, at "[tying] up heavy burdens and lay[ing] them on men's shoulders, but they themselves are unwilling to move them with so much as a finger" (Matt. 23:4).

When Judas shows up on their doorstep, these connivers must feel as if they've won the lottery. They finally have what they've prayed for: an insider who will deliver Jesus to them, a man so furious with Jesus' refusal to play the political savior that he's finished with Him—he wants Him taken out. Judas is the perfect answer to the double riddle confounding the Jewish religious leaders—how can they capture Jesus far away from the rabid crowds that have dogged Him while simultaneously pinning the blame on a fall guy they can finger after the fact? It's as if the heavens have dropped a miracle into their well-fed, tasseled laps. And, of course, they are thanking God for their good fortune—after all, the good are rewarded with what they deserve and the bad are punished with what they fear....

Scene 2: Jesus' disciples must find a Passover gathering place by following His quirky, unnecessarily bizarre instructions.

To Peter and John, Jesus says with what I picture an impish smile on His face, "Keep your eyes open as you enter [Jerusalem]. A man carrying a water jug will meet you. Follow him home. Then speak with the owner of the house: The Teacher wants to know, 'Where is the guest room where I can eat the Passover meal with my disciples?' He will show you a spacious second-story room, swept and ready. Prepare the meal there" (Luke 22:10–12 MSG).

Really?

Stalk the guy with the water jug, follow him home, barge in behind him, and inform the homeowner that "the Teacher" is planning to use his spare room for a Passover party? Is all this embarrassing gamesmanship really necessary? It's as if Jesus is always and everywhere playfully reminding His close friends that, like Superman, He hails from another planet. "This is how we do it on Krypton (aka the kingdom of God)...."

In the end, nothing separates "natural" from "supernatural" in Jesus' reality or His vocabulary or His party-planning sensibilities—all things are both/and....

- The sea is natural, but the walking on it is supernatural.
- The food is natural, but its vast multiplication is supernatural.

- The fishing advice is natural, but the catch is supernatural.
- The water is natural, but the process of converting it into wine is supernatural.
- The conversation on the Mount of Transfiguration is supernatural, but the prophets' words of advice are natural.
- The paralyzed limb is natural, but the limb restored is supernatural.
- The demons are supernatural, but the voice that calmly demands that they leave is natural.
- The storm is natural, but the command that calms it is supernatural.

And so, for Jesus, which is easier—to ask His disciples to secure a room in the natural way, or to ask them to secure a room by *acting on* His supernatural instructions? Well, like the children He so loved to be near, "the road less traveled" for Jesus is always the road to the swing set; He chooses the playful over the grindstone.

Scene 3: Jesus speaks tenderly to His disciples, embracing their friendship and savoring His last meal with them while reminding them of the suffering He's about to endure.

If you had one last meal with your friends—the people who know you best but are oblivious to the horror you're about to endure—what would you say to them as you scan their faces at the table? Well, this is what Jesus says: "You've no idea how much I have looked forward to eating this Passover meal with you before I enter my time of suffering.

It's the last one I'll eat until we all it eat together in the kingdom of God" (Luke 22:14–16 MSG). He loves these guys, and He's grateful they're with Him before all hell breaks loose, literally…. And buried under His ominous reminder about "my time of suffering" He tosses a little hope their way: "until we all eat it together in the kingdom of God." We will, He assures, meet again…. It's Hawkeye, in *The Last of the Mohicans*, explaining to his great love, Cora, that in order to save her life he must abandon her in their cave hideout to a vicious war party of Hurons, with the hope that they will merely capture, not kill her. He can save her only by leaving her first—it is not the end of their romance, he assures: "Submit, do you hear? Be strong! Survive! Stay alive no matter what occurs. I will find you, no matter how long it takes, no matter how far. I will find you."[2]

Scene 4: He passes around bread and wine—symbols of the Passover, the intervention of God to redeem His children—and tells them it's His flesh and blood, given wholly for them.

No more lamb's blood, used as a temporary substitute for the blood of God. Now it's Jesus' very own blood painted on the doorpost that will save them. The sacrificial lamb they're eating is the last time—*the very last time*—any Jew anywhere will need to ingest these foods as a stand-in for the propitiation for their sins. Soon, they will be invited to ingest Jesus Himself through the infilling of the Holy Spirit. They feast this day on their friend, not yet understanding how, apart from cannibalism, He will get from *there* to *here*. All of Jesus' confusing, disturbing, and offensive demands that they "eat His body" and "drink His blood" will soon make sense—not long from now they will abandon the dead meat of a sacrificed lamb for the living flesh of Jesus, what He calls "living bread," "true food," and "true drink" (John 6). They will eat of Him and live forever.

Scene 5: He tells them that one who eats with Him at the table is about to betray Him.

In that upper room, Jesus' matter-of-fact accusation functions like the pulled pin from a grenade—the room is plunged into dread and confusion. The disciples' response is perfectly human. In low tones they assess the one "most likely to betray," morphing their celebration into a kind of kangaroo court. There are no heroics here—no one throws himself on the grenade. But all are quick to nominate others for the job.

Scene 6: The disciples then argue about who is "regarded" as the greatest among them.

Of course, the transition from accusation into argument makes perfect sense—one feeds the other. The same evidence that acquits me of betrayal must also convict me of transcendence. And if it seems crazy that mere men would dicker about their relative greatness while God sits a few feet away with a bemused smile on His face, then you don't know yourself well. We are all, fundamentally, obsessively concerned about our own guilt and innocence—even as the Lamb of God offers His innocence in trade for our guilt. That deal matters to us, but not usually in the moment of our unveiled guilt. We first default to homemade remedies that promise to cure our guilt: our comparative goodness, our excuses, and our denial. Only when we exhaust our normal appeals do we typically turn to God and begrudgingly settle for what C. S. Lewis, in *The Great Divorce*, calls "the bleeding charity."[3]

Scene 7: Jesus tells his brothers that their view of greatness is not only back-ward but offensive in light of His own example of servanthood.

The voice of the Lion of the tribe of Judah booms over the chaos created by His warring disciples—toddlers in a sandbox throwing sand at each other—by redefining greatness on His own terms. The Master plays the servant, even as the servants try on His crown for size. That won't do, He reminds them—they will not use their association with Him to lord it over anyone. *Anyone.* In fact, their silly little arguments will soon be dwarfed by the real responsibilities of greatness—they will, He promises, "sit on thrones judging the twelve tribes of Israel." Greatness has little to do with the typical way we assess status; instead, it wins us the prize of greater and greater expectations. So, for instance, your name might be Kennedy, but you'll have to pay for it by giving up your life.

Scene 8: Jesus then pulls the pin on a second and much more devastating grenade.

Now Jesus is ready to change everything—now He will utter "The Seven Sentence Fragments That Will Change the World." Now He gets nose to nose with Peter to say something that will change every-thing for him and for us. Satan, He begins, has paid Him a visit....

What if, when you spoke, every word *perfectly represented* perfect truth? What if you could compress all the collected wisdom of the world into a single word symbol? What if your strength—the same strength that spawned a universe most physicists believe is infinitely expanding, where light from the farthest object we've ever detected took thirteen billion years to reach earth—was all brought to bear in three sentences, seven fragments, one fifteen-second engagement? What if your words were like wells instead of spoons? What if you could use your words to amputate and regenerate in the same swift motion?

Well, you'd be Jesus.

And you could say your three sentences—your seven sentence fragments—and leave them there for us to dip our buckets into, over and over. Because the water in those wells will give us life, just as He slyly promised the Samaritan woman: "Jesus answered her, 'If you knew the gift of God and who it is that asks you for a drink, you would have asked him and he would have given you living water'" (John 4:10 NIV). Every word Jesus speaks comes from the same spring that created the universe—each one has an infinite capacity for truth. There is nothing wasted and nothing left out from His discourse. Charles H. Spurgeon says: "They used to say of certain mines in Cornwall that the deeper you went the richer was the ore; assuredly is it so with the mines of inspired Scripture."[4] This is a metaphorical statement that represents a literal truth, not a rhetorical one. It means that we can drill and drill and drill deep into each sentence, phrase, and word to find His bottomless truths. And what we find is wholly dependent on how deep we're willing to go.… So grab a flashlight and a spade and let's start digging, because the "richer gold" waits for those who will dirty up their hands.

"Simon, Simon, Satan has asked to sift you as wheat. But I have prayed for you, Simon, that your faith may not fail. And when you have turned back, strengthen your brothers."

CHAPTER 1

"SIMON, SIMON ..."

(Jesus Calls Us by Names)

Where were You
When everything was falling apart?
All my days
Were spent by the telephone.
It never rang.
—From "You Found Me" by The Fray[1]

What have I become?
My sweetest friend...
If I could start again
A million miles away
I would keep myself
I would find a way
—From "Hurt" by Trent Reznor of Nine Inch Nails[2]

The names we're bound to are far more powerful than we realize....

Not long ago I saw the award-winning and farcical short film *Validation*—it's about a nondescript man stationed at a nondescript parking-validation kiosk in the nondescript lot below a nondescript building who changes the whole world merely because he understands the profound impact of naming people well.[3] One by one, he greets the parade of lost souls who trudge up to his kiosk with something true and grand about who they are. He studies them closely, sees them well, then quickly projects onto them their forgotten beauty. One is a girl with beautiful eyes, another surely has wisdom beyond her years, still another is far more talented than he's given credit for, and yet another (a bit of a stretch) exhibits remarkable sartorial taste. Each person arrives at the kiosk with a barely detectable pulse—all the life sucked out of them by a world that names them harshly, with systematic and brutal impunity. And each person leaves, moments later, like an inflated balloon, full of their own essence and daring to hope again. It's not long before city leaders, then world leaders, beg the man for private meetings, and his exploits are plastered across newspapers in every country. By describing people as they truly are, not as their interior voices accuse them, he literally breathes life into dead souls.

But not everyone is so receptive. The girl who takes the driver's license photos at the DMV refuses to open herself to the beautiful names he throws at her. And she's offended by his repeated transgressions against the DMV's central rule for license photos: "Absolutely no smiling." She simply won't believe anything—*anything*—true about herself. Her smile is locked away in a dark cell, and there is no key. She is the rock he crashes his boat into, over and over, until his soul is punctured and he finally sinks into despair.

In the wake of this devastation he loses his own name—hopelessness overtakes him, and he heartily agrees with the cynical voices inside him that rail against the futile way he's lived his life. All of this renders him powerless to name others. The crowds that used to line up at his kiosk disappear, shrinking away from the man's glum new mantra: "This is probably as good as it's going to get for you." He wanders the city, lost and separated from his true identity.

Then, by a fluke, the man begins taking photos of tourists when they ask—and he finds he can't restrain himself from naming their beautiful smiles, their obvious virtues, and their happy fortunes. He rediscovers his soul and begins carrying a camera with him everywhere, stopping to take photos of passersby, treating them as if they are royalty. He asks a ravaged woman, dour and confined to a wheelchair, what makes her happy. "My daughter's smile," she says, smiling for the first time in years. And he snaps her picture. "You have a beautiful smile," he names.

One day, when he's delivering an armful of film to be developed at a one-hour photo shop, he runs smack into the DMV girl of his dreams, the same one whose refusal to smile dismantled his soul. She is snapping passport photos for a long line of takers—and she is smiling and radiant. He watches as she names and "validates" the next person in line. And he is undone again. What could account for this impossible resurrection? She shows him a photo of her mother, explaining that her mother hasn't smiled for years since a devastating accident confined her to a wheelchair. In the photo, she is smiling. He knows the woman well, because he took the first picture of her smile. He looks up with tears in his eyes, and the girl is smiling. And the truth dawns on him. The mother's smile is the redemptive key to the girl's cell door. The girl's smile (and her true identity) walks out of the shadows into the light. She has quit her job to search for him and offer her thanks. Standing there, surrounded by the newly named, she pledges her love and lights his face with her radiance. His naming in her life, like a rushing flood, has finally carved out a new tributary. She is reborn. And she returns the grace by naming the one who has named everyone.

I'm sure the filmmakers had no intention of crafting a contemporary metaphor for the tipping-point encounter between Jesus and Peter in Matthew 16, but that's how God rolls (when the Pharisees, in Luke 19, demand that the disciples stop praising Jesus as their "king," Jesus responds: "I tell you, if these become silent, the stones will cry out" [v. 40]). God will tell His own version of His redemptive story by any means possible. And Jesus names us to redeem us, and, in turn, we name Him:

> Now when Jesus came into the district of Caesarea Philippi, He was asking His disciples, "Who do people say that the Son of Man is?" And they said, "Some say John the Baptist; and others, Elijah; but still others, Jeremiah, or one of the prophets." He said to them, "But who do you say that I am?" Simon Peter answered, "You are the Christ, the Son of the living God." And Jesus said to him, "Blessed are you, Simon Barjona, because flesh and blood did not reveal this to you, but My Father who is in heaven. I also say to you that you are Peter, and upon this rock I will build My church; and the gates of Hades will not overpower it." (Matt. 16:13–18)

The message here is simple and profound—and forgotten, most often:

The names we embrace are the names we become,
therefore ...
we're in desperate need of a good name.
And this:
Jesus will name us as we name Him....

Can You Hear Me Now?

My full name is Richard Allen Lawrence, and even now as I type
these three names I can hear my mom's voice, far off.but piercing the
air, calling me home from my adventures as a boy. You and I know
exactly what it means when our moms call us *by all three names*—
we've done something big and bad. If we're lucky, we remember what
that big/bad thing is as we huff/puff toward home. If we're unlucky,
she will surprise us. One thing is sure, when we're children our moms
never treat our formal names casually—they use our full names to
get our attention. That's basically the function of our formal names:
to rivet our attention.

It's important to remember this as Jesus transitions from
His "Servanthood 101" lecture and turns to face Peter. It's a big
moment—He needs his friend's full attention. It's time to use his
formal name. There are other instances in Luke when Peter is refer-
enced by his formal name, and they are all big moments:

- In Luke 5 Jesus climbs into *Simon's* fishing boat
  and uses it as a floating platform for one of His
  first sermons, later directing the incredulous fisherman to drop his nets on a huge catch and calling
  him into a new occupation—"fisher of men."

- In Luke 6 Jesus formally chooses His twelve disciples, including *Simon*.
- In Luke 7 Jesus pulls *Simon* aside to show him the difference between desperate love and cautious support—he compares the weeping, foot-kissing, perfume-anointing behavior of a forgiven prostitute to the proper formality of *Simon* and those gathered in his home.
- And, finally, in Luke 24 when the disciples have recongregated in Jerusalem to compare notes on whether Jesus had actually risen from the dead, the proof they offer is that He "has appeared to *Simon*" (v. 34).

Simon's full name is Simon Barjona, or Simon son of Jonah. Leading into His "sifting" revelation, Jesus addresses him by his formal name to capture his attention and communicate an overarching truth: "I know who you are—I know everything about you. And it's time to pay attention to Me." He's reaching Peter at his core by using the name that represents his history on earth—his parents, siblings, occupation, and accomplishments. It's both formal and intimate, the same way an affectionate Jesus, in Luke 10, gently rebukes His good friend: "'Martha, Martha,' the Lord answered, 'you are worried and upset about many things, but only one thing is needed. Mary has chosen what is better, and it will not be taken away from her'" (vv. 41–42 NIV). With Martha, as with Peter in the upper room, He repeats His friend's name twice to drive home an intimate truth: "I love you, and I have something hard to say to you...." Jesus is

establishing an enveloping connection, the kind that's always delivered close in, with direct eye contact.

"Do I have your attention now?"

The man attached to the name Simon Barjona is a fisherman
from Bethsaida, called "the fishers town," situated on the northern
tip of the Sea of Galilee in the land of Jesus' boyhood. He is the
tough and driven owner of a small business at a time when most
of the people around him work as slaves. Replace the bumbling,
stumbling picture you have of him in your mind with the picture of
a man rough and big and calloused and savvy—a man to contend
with. A young Clint Eastwood. And on the day he meets Jesus he is,
like most small-business owners, hard at work, oblivious to the man
he will later die for.

That's when Jesus, pressed to the water's edge by the gathering
crowd, jumps into one of two empty boats hauled up on the shore—
they are both owned by Simon. So Jesus, already presumptuous in
His trespass, asks Simon to jump in with Him and push out into
the water. The exhausted man has just finished another grueling
all-nighter on the choppy sea, with nothing to show for his dirty,
dangerous labor. He must finish washing and mending his nets
before he can go home and sleep. The last thing he wants to do is
get back in that boat and push out into the water. But he's caught up
in the moment and by the crowds and by the invitation. And when
Jesus is finished speaking He smiles at Simon, and, like that uncle
who loves to amaze your kids with his clever little "magic" tricks, He
pulls something out of his hat: "Put out into the deep water and let
down your nets for a catch" (Luke 5:4). It's not the more cautious
"let down your nets" that rouses Simon's ire; it's the "for a catch"

chutzpah. "Master, we worked hard all night and caught nothing, but at Your bidding I will let down the nets."

Humor this guy, get Him out of my stupid boat, go home.

It is the perfect, playful miracle. So many fish swarm into Simon's nets that he screams for the crew of the other boat to push out and help with the catch. The nets strain and the boats start to sink under their load. And what is Jesus doing as the fish pour into the boat? Scripture doesn't say, but I imagine His laughter booms and ricochets over the water as He stands, hands on hips, at the back of the boat. It's all play to Him. But it drops Simon to his knees as if he's been shot. He is not a rhetorical man; he's a man who does and does and does—driven by compelling momentum, decisive and forceful. So, while others are marveling at the Man's feat, Simon is groveling at His feet: "Depart from me, for I am a sinful man, O Lord!" (Luke 5:8 NKJV). It is the first recorded act of repentance in response to Jesus, and the first in a long string of firsts for Peter. He is …

- the first to be called by Jesus;
- the first to follow Jesus;
- the first to publicly name Jesus as Messiah;
- the first to be renamed by Jesus;
- the first (other than Jesus) to walk on water;
- the first to use violence to defend Jesus when he draws his sword in the garden of Gethsemane;
- the first to walk into Jesus' empty tomb;
- the first to reach Jesus on the shores of the Sea of Tiberias after His resurrection;

- the first to preach about Jesus in the public square; and
- the first to lead the church of Jesus Christ.

These "firsts" define a man used to winning and overcoming—quitting is anathema to him. And that's why every time Jesus talks about His impending death, Simon is the one vigorously protesting. "Jesus killed? Not on my watch…." There's that Clint Eastwood squint. After he names Jesus the "Messiah, the son of the living God" in front of the other disciples, Jesus immediately returns the favor and names him Petros, "the rock," or Peter—it's a Greek word never before used as a name. Soon after, he briefly earns another nickname—"Satan," or the "adversary"—because Peter's fixation on winning blinds him to Jesus' mission and purpose. His moxie is the reason he's chosen, and it's the reason he's about to be sifted.

It's so important to remember the makeup of this man—otherwise, all that happens next is lost on us. "Simon Barjona" represents all the man has been; "Peter" represents all he truly is. One is the name of his first birth; the other is the name of his second birth.

Sitting Bull, Gideon, and a Boy Named Sue

Native Americans most closely resemble the ancient Jews in the way they name their children—they craft names to *project* more than to *reflect*. For example, Anaba means "she returns from battle," Oneida means "eagerly awaited," Chesmu means "gritty," and Dyami means "soaring eagle." The Jews do likewise. For example, Jacob means "he who supplants," and he did. Abram means "high father," and he was. Sarah means "princess," and she was. Gideon means "valiant warrior," and he was. Yeshua means "Savior," and, of course, He is.

In the Old Testament book of Hosea, naming is the central theme—it's a parable for what Brennan Manning calls "the furious longing of God."[4] When God commands the prophet to marry a prostitute named Gomer, He also tells Hosea to name two of his children as stand-in symbols of the curse He's put upon all of wayward Israel—one is to be called Lo-ruhamah, which means "she has not obtained compassion," and the other is to be called Lo-ammi, which means "not my people." Then, as a sign and symbol of the redemptive love that will unravel the dire offenses of a people who have rejected Him and played the harlot, God tells Hosea to rename his cursed children. The first becomes Ruhamah, or "she has obtained compassion," and the second becomes Ammi, or "my people." Born under a curse, reborn under a promise. This cycle is the deepest rhythm in Peter's life, and in our own.

Most often, the people you know who've either changed their names or longed to do it are thirsty for a rebirth—a redemption that will help them escape their own private curse.

My wife, Beverly Rose, was named by her mother after her half-sister (Beverly) and her mother (Rose). My wife's grandmother Rose had three children, then divorced their father. Before she remarried, the state sent all three to an orphanage because there was no food in the house when social workers arrived to check on the children. Carmella, Bev's mother, was five at the time. After Rose married again, she and her new husband had two daughters of their own. Carmella lived at that orphanage run by nuns until she was fourteen, when her mother called the nuns and demanded that Carmella get on a train that would bring her to the home that was never her home—that very day. Though she pleaded with the nuns, she was not allowed to go to her eighth-grade graduation party that night; instead, she boarded a train to meet a woman she'd not seen since she was a preschooler. Leaving the only home she knew through a veil of tears, Carmella arrived at her mother's home, feeling like a second-class child—one who was expected to channel Cinderella and serve the family. She was told she was the "lucky one" because her stepfather had agreed to take her in. The class system she then lived under haunted her the rest of her life. And that's why, when she gave birth to her second daughter, she decided to name her "Beverly" as a kind of appeasement to the "gods" who were her half sisters, and she gave her the middle name "Rose" as an offering at the altar of her own mom. This was Carmella's way of trying to win favor with her mother and her half sister—the favor she had never tasted as a free gift. So "Beverly," far from a projection of beauty, was her mom's futile way of bargaining with her half sisters for their love. And Bev, like Lo-ruhamah and Lo-ammi before her, has ever since longed to be free of that curse.

That's because the names we embrace are the names we become.

"Simon, Simon" is Jesus' way of cornering the man still veiled by the husk of the curse. Our given names may reflect something true about our first-birth identities, and they will certainly exert a kind of forming influence over our souls, but they are not the names that best describe who we really are. From my perspective, my wife has transcended the cursed genesis of her name—*Beverly* means "beauty" to me. But, for her, the name still exerts a kind of insidious influence over her life, even to this day. Those who know us well are *not* surprised to learn that we labored and wrestled and fretted over the names we chose for our two girls—Lucy and Emma. As with many of our decisions, we tortured our way to a final choice. In the end we named Lucy after the bold younger sister in *The Lion, the Witch, and the Wardrobe*, and we named Emma after the headstrong Jane Austen heroine (and because it sounded Victorian). I think we did our best to thoughtfully project an attractive identity for both our girls—they have grown into their names. But I'm certain that these are not the names that best describe them, because our perspective on their God-given identities is myopic—we're likely playing Russian roulette with their identities whenever we name our kids.

The Johnny Cash song "A Boy Named Sue" tells the brutal story of a father who inexplicably bestows a girl's name upon his infant son, then disappears from his life. After years of hardship and struggle (the boy learns to use his fists and his wits to survive the abuse poured on him because of his name) he tracks down the father he has vowed to kill and spews his bitterness: "My name is 'Sue!' How do you do! Now you're gonna die!" The ensuing brawl ends with the son pointing a gun at his "big and bent and gray and old" father. The battered, bleeding man stares back at his son and, smiling, says: "Son, this world is rough. And if a man's gonna make it, he's gotta be tough. And I knew I wouldn't be there to help ya along. So I give ya that name and I said good-bye.… I know you hate me, and you got the right to kill me now.… But ya ought to thank me, before I die, for the gravel in ya guts and the spit in ya eye."[5] The name, indeed, formed the boy—but formed him into what? A brawling, despondent, vengeful young man who moved from town to town all his life "to hide my shame." You have to wonder if the father would've been wiser to name the boy "Richard the Lion-Hearted" instead—but that wouldn't pass muster as a country song. The point is that the father intended to *form* his son by naming him; his cruelty was an intentional attempt to guarantee his son's survival.

The names we embrace are the names we become.

The forming power of naming is unmistakable and more saturating than we realize, and it's not hard to find examples. There are two middle-aged brothers in my church whose last name, for most of their lives, was literally "Failyer." For years they labored through life, their families burdened by the latent curse of their surname. Not long ago, after their wives had pressed them for years to look into changing their name, the men decided to research the origins of "Failyer" and discovered it's an Americanized version of their original German surname—Fehler. When they formally adopted the German original as their last name, it's as if the sun rose over their families' landscape.

The names we embrace are the names we become.

Entering into Your Aragorn Moment

In J. R. R. Tolkien's epic conclusion to the Lord of the Rings saga, *The Return of the King*, the man who's spent his life as a shadowy ranger, the man who calls himself Strider, refuses to step into his true name—Aragorn, the king of Gondor. Aragorn is heir to an ancient lineage that has always formed a bulwark against the forces of evil, but he can't accept his true name because he is hobbled by the shame he feels over the onetime cowardice of his ancestors. He is living under a curse. So he has stubbornly held onto his identity as "Strider" because there are no expectations attached to it—as Strider, he can remain in the shadows, full of grand promise but isolated and neutered. He's afraid to step into his mythic identity and become what he was meant to be.

And that's when a wise old warrior arrives, in secret, to call him out. Strider is summoned to a tent where he sees King Théoden of Rohan talking with a hooded figure, the elven Lord Elrond. Elrond is there to see Aragorn, not Strider, because the ranger's refusal to embrace his true identity is paving the way for the forces of wickedness to spread unchecked in the land. The evil lord Sauron is massing an army of killers so vast and fearsome that it may already be too late for a stand. From behind his back Elrond produces the sheathed sword called Andúril—a legendary weapon wielded by the great kings of Gondor and formerly shattered in battle. Elven craftsmen have reforged the blade in secret. I'll let the film's screenplay pick up the story:

> **Aragorn:** *(Takes the sword, staring at it in wonder)* Sauron will not have forgotten the sword of Elendil. *(He draws the long blade from its sheath)* The blade that was broken shall return to Minas Tirith.
>
> **Elrond:** *(Intently)* The man who can wield the power of this sword can summon to him an army more deadly than any that walks this earth. *(Stares hard at Aragorn)* Put aside the Ranger—become

who you were born to be.... *(A heavy silence hangs in the room)*[6]

Elrond's appeal works. When Strider leaves the tent he is Aragorn—he has, as Elrond has demanded, "put aside the Ranger." He will go on to embrace the mantle of king and lead the forces of good to victory over Sauron and the forces of darkness. When is the pinpoint moment when the pendulum of history swings toward the good and away from the evil? It is, of course, when Elrond challenges Strider to step into his true name and identity—Aragorn.

Have you had your own Aragorn moment?

Has God ever answered this deepest-of-all question in your life?

You know your given name, but do you know the name of your rebirth?

In Revelation 2:17 Jesus, speaking to His disciples, says: "To him who overcomes, to him I will give some of the hidden manna, and I will give him a white stone, and a new name written on the stone which no one knows but he who receives it." Whatever's written on that stone, it's a name God has chosen for you, to project on to you your mission and purpose in life, just as He chose Petros to supersede, not supplant, Simon. And He will reveal this white-stone name to you alone first—it is one of His greatest acts of intimacy.

My own "Aragorn moment" is seared in my heart—it is as grand and infused with import as that scene in *The Return of the King*, because the forces of darkness in my life were routed when it looked as if they were about to win. It was early in my marriage. I was a featured speaker at a youth ministry conference—the last place I wanted to be at that moment in my life. The arguments that were typical of our early marriage relationship had entered into new territory—I wasn't sure we could escape the cycle of wounding. We were both prisoners of our mistaken identities; I believed there was a hollow place where my soul should've been, and that belief was destroying the love we had for each other. When I left our home for the conference, Bev's icy silence had the smell of death to me. I could tell what had just happened between us was way beyond our typical patterns of recovery-and-forgiveness followed by a slow thaw. As I boarded the plane, I felt as if I was standing in the queue for the electric chair; I'd have given anything for a hint of mercy. I arrived at the hotel and immediately found a quiet place to call her. She answered, heard my voice, and hung up. I did this repeatedly, like a man insane. Every abrupt end to my call was like a dagger jammed and twisted into my gut.

So I walked through the halls of the convention center with a soul dazed and bludgeoned, hoping no one would recognize me so I wouldn't have to play the poser. I crept close to the walls—a man afraid to show himself. The voices inside were thick with accusation and criticism. I felt like throwing up. It was during one of these wall-hugging journeys down a crowded hallway that I felt God beckoning me. If He had suddenly appeared before me I would not have been surprised—His voice was so urgent and magnetic. I looked around for someplace to "meet" Him, and an unlocked door led me to a darkened, empty conference room. I somehow knew to pull out a legal pad to write down what He was about to say to me. I sat on the floor, with the pad on my lap, waiting. And then His voice came like a lightning bolt. I had to write fast just to keep up. I didn't even process what He said to me until after His voice fell silent—the

transcription was all I could handle at first. And then, when I'd read
it for the first time, it was as if paramedics had jolted me with those
electrified paddles that kick-start your heart.

. He did nothing to calm my fears or predict an easy reconciliation; instead, He described what was there in that hollow place
where my soul was supposed to be, using a metaphorical name for
me that is so deeply intimate, it still brings tears to my eyes as I type
these words. Here's what I transcribed:

> You're a quarterback. You see the field. You're
> squirming away from the rush to find space to
> release the ball. You never give up. You have cour-
> age in the face of ferocity—in fact, ferocity draws
> out your courage. You want to score even when the
> team is too far behind for it to matter. You love the
> thrill of creating a play in the huddle, under pres-
> sure, and spreading the ball around to everyone on
> the team. You have no greater feeling than throwing
> the ball hard to a spot and watching the receiver
> get to it without breaking stride. In fact, you love
> it most when the receiver is closely covered and it
> takes a perfect throw to get it to him. You have the
> same feeling when you throw a bomb and watch
> the receiver run under it, or when you tear away
> from the grasp of a defender, or when you see and
> feel blood on your elbows or knees and feel alive
> because of it. You love to score right after the other
> team has scored, but you want to do it methodically,

first down by first down, right down the field. You
love fourth down! You want to win but are satisfied
by fighting well.

The affect of this message to me—sitting alone on the floor of an
empty conference room—was as if I'd been yanked out of the torrent.
I cried and cried and cried until I couldn't cry anymore. At my most
desperate hour, the Lord Jesus saved me by naming me, just as He
did for Peter. With "Simon, Simon" He spoke to the man as he was,
marking the moment before the sifting freed him from his imprison-
ing husk. With "Peter" He gave him a life vest he could cling to as
the flood of his sifting carried him through the worst nights and days
of his life. While "Rick" sums up my history, "Quarterback" sums
up my nature: the truth about my heart and identity. God never uses
duct tape to fix things—He will take your flesh and blood if you offer
it to Him and use it like Play-Doh: "Behold, I will do a new thing,
now it shall spring forth; shall you not know it?" (Isa. 43:19 NKJV). I
did know it, in the calm after my storm.

When I returned home, my wife stood a few feet from me and
spoke from a thousand miles away—she asked for a separation: "I'd
like you out of the house by tonight." I moved into the basement
apartment of a coworker, and later the basement apartment of a
friend. I spent the holidays apart from her, crying all the time as the
husk of my false identity loosened under the assault of my sifting.
I reminded myself of "Quarterback" as I lay down on the threshing floor and spread my arms wide—helpless to stop the pounding,
holding on to Him as a shipwrecked man clings to the only piece of
floating wreckage he can find.

And then, a few months later, in the middle of an appointment with our counselor, Carl, the husk finally fell away. One moment I was describing the emptiness that was "Rick" before my naming experience at the conference, and the next I was bursting into uncontrollable, soul-shaking sobs as Carl bolted across the room to kneel in front of me, his face just inches from mine, his flashing eyes locked on mine: "Rick, your soul is full, and you are loved." These words uncorked something primal in me. I rushed from the room ready to vomit up the bile that had simmered in my soul for a quarter century. I drove a few blocks away and parked by an empty field, where my sobs shook the car and I felt my first taste of freedom. I could barely walk after this experience. A few weeks later I moved back into our home and, like the parent of a newborn, started to get to know the truth about myself for the first time. And I discovered, like the man in *Validation*, that finding my own name gave me the foundation and courage to name others.

"Quarterback" is no mere affirmation, just as a wedding is no mere date. Affirmation makes us feel good about who we are. Naming reveals our true nature. We pay attention when God calls us by our given name, cling to Him while we are being sifted, then embrace the name that is truly ours on the other side. This is exactly what Peter did.

Is it possible that we all have two names—the one our parents gave us, and the one that God calls us when He's plotting His next adventure? Is it possible that He uses our formal name, as He did with Peter, to get our attention—to speak to our history, to prepare us for the sifting that will separate us from the husk of our identity? Is it possible He wouldn't mind if we asked Him who we really are, just so we know what will be left over after the sifting? Because sifting will reveal us—the *me* that's been broken and broken and broken until it almost can't be found, and the *me* we have been since our good Father formed us in the womb. The "true name" He has chosen for each of us perfectly represents the *revealed me* that emerges through our sifting.

In my speaking ministry I often invite people to "ask the question"—I mean, I ask them to find a place in our meeting room where they can feel alone, then to simply pursue God for an answer to the question Jesus first asked His disciples: "Who do you say I am?" (Matt. 16:15 NIV). I first coach them to take authority over their own voice and the voice of God's Enemy.[7] Literally, I ask them to tell their own voice to be silent and to remind Satan and his demonic host that they have no freedom to speak. Then I invite them to ask the question and wait—to resist their fundamental impatience. Sometimes I ask them to open wide their arms as a physical expression of their openness to God's voice. And I always ask them to write what they see or hear or sense. In those sacred ten minutes, some come away with nothing—it's not their time. And some come away with everything, and nothing is ever the same again. They are *found,* many for the first time in their lives.

One of those is Rebecca, who sent me this note today:

> When you talked about asking God to tell us our new name as we name Him—like Peter did with naming Jesus and then Jesus gave him a new name—the name that God gave me was 'Transmitter." Hearing my new name was very cool to me! My first thoughts were, however: "Transmitter"? Why not a prettier name like "Radio" or whatever?' Then I quickly stopped myself and thanked God for

answering me. I know God has used me to share messages with others before, and He knows He has placed me in a ministry that is not what I would have chosen for myself—I did not envision myself working with youth. The attacks on our family are often heavy and relentless. But through Christ alone, we press forward. I have a feeling that this whole Transmitter name will continue to make more and more sense as I walk along with Christ.[8]

After a "naming" experience such as Rebecca's, I ask people to choose a discerning spiritual leader and show him or her what they've written—to ask for an honest reaction. I encourage them to start telling their close and trusted circle of friends what they now know about themselves. The day I shared my naming experience with my friend Bob Krulish, the director of pastoral staff at my church, was the day he started referencing it in every email (often closing with "Throw long!") and in most conversations ("Way to quarterback that!"). This has had a profound impact on me—like bathing in the deepest truths about my soul.

The experience of asking God to reveal our second-birth name is a volatile act of faith—we need a community of people who will confirm and undergird and even edit this experience for us. The community guarantees that the naming will be treated as sacred, commanding the same respect that we give to the birthing process. Author and pastor Walter Wangerin says there are, universally, two "creation" languages. The first is spoken by God, who "spoke everything into being" out of nothing at all. The second is the language He first gave to Adam—the language of naming (Gen. 2). Names, says Wangerin, are not merely labels: "The thing named is brought into place so it can be known. A name establishes a person's relationship with other named things. The naming action begins to declare the person's purpose. And this naming is powerful, but also dangerous."[9]

Naming, truly, *is* powerful and dangerous. Damning, accusing words or descriptions are, of course, not from God. Normal parents never describe the essence of their children with words that damn. Never. We already know what's wrong with us—we know it very well. But we know very little about what's right with us, the person God has said is "fearfully and wonderfully made" (Ps. 139:14). Maybe you already know whether God is pressing you to ask Him the question. It's not a mark of immaturity if it's not time, and it's not a mark of maturity if it is. It's God who knows your real name, and it's God who will reveal it to you if He wants to. In Isaiah 43:1 He promises: "Do not fear, for I have redeemed you; I have called you by name; you are Mine!"

These are the sweetest words we'll ever hear in life.

Beauty Will Rise

On May 21, 2008, Steven Curtis Chapman's oldest son accidentally drove over his five-year-old sister in the driveway of their home, killing her instantly. Chapman, an award-winning singer/songwriter who lives every day in the public eye, was then forced to live out an intolerable grief in the spotlight. Just a few days before the darkest day in their lives, the entire Chapman family was in China when a 7.9 magnitude earthquake dismantled the Sichuan province, a mountainous region in the western portion of the country. They were in the Shanghai airport hundreds of miles away from the epicenter, headed home to celebrate Maria Sue Chapman's fifth birthday. Only five years before, China had been her home. She was one of three Chinese orphan girls adopted by the Chapmans. At the airport waiting for their flight, they didn't even feel the quake. But they personally knew many of those who now had to cope with the massive physical and personal destruction—they had spent four weeks in Sichuan province in support of an aid agency.

I'd heard the basic details of all of this, as did the millions around the world who respect Chapman and enjoy his music. And then, a year or so later, a prerelease CD of Chapman's new album landed on my desk. I get several of these every day because the magazine I've headed for more than twenty years runs music reviews. I'd never been a rabid fan of Chapman's music, I have to admit. But something about this album's cover was drilling into my soul. On it, you see Chapman standing on the precipice of a deep gorge, arms raised, face caught up in ecstasy, with his guitar slung over his shoulder. At first I thought the background behind him was a mountain range. But when I looked closer I could see that it was actually a mountain of rubble. I read the liner notes and discovered Chapman was standing near a leveled village in the Chinese quake zone. He'd returned to China about a year after his daughter's death to minister to those who'd survived their own trauma, helping open an orphan care center named after Maria and offering a free concert to the grieving families of earthquake victims. The title of the album precisely matched the photo on its cover: *Beauty Will Rise*.

The photo is such a perfect metaphor for Chapman's sifting experience—plain evidence of the catastrophic in the background, the worship of the free in the foreground. I couldn't stop staring at this photo—even now it rivets me, and new metaphors surface. In the photo he's standing on the edge of doom, a pinpoint of rock jutting into the dark chasm of rubble that drops hundreds of feet below him. It is a visual treatise on the reality and the promise of our own sifting experiences. Chapman's dangerous act of worship is just as jolting, just as contradictory, just as haunting, and just as beautiful as the songs of grief on the album. How is it possible to worship God when the worst thing we can imagine happens to us?

"Do not fear, for I have redeemed you; I have called you by name; you are Mine!"

Maybe "the arrow that flies by day"[10] will find its mark in us—maybe an innocent little girl will die on our driveway, maybe a hero will die a pauper. And maybe we'll emerge from all of it with a ridiculous thirst to worship God, because He's named us and claimed us in the darkness of our sifting. When I was growing up, the "name it and claim it" theology was all the rage—it thrived because it perfectly fit the unique narcissism of an American culture that treats prayer like a bank robber's note to the teller. "Name it and claim it" has now largely been scorned to death—but not in the kingdom of heaven, where the Father, Son, and Holy Spirit are delightedly working around the clock to name and claim all who will rejoin their family. The last lines in Chapman's song "God Is in Control," as he grieves over a great sadness that is not as it "should be" or "could be," offer an exclamation point on how it "will be", when…

We finally will see
We'll see with our own eyes
He was always in control
And we'll sing holy, holy, holy is our God
And we will finally really understand what it means[11]

CHAPTER 2

"SATAN HAS ASKED ..."

(Jesus in Conversation with the Enemy)

Take heed to yourselves because the tempter will make
his first and sharpest assault on you. If you will be
leaders against him, he will not spare you. He bears
the greatest malice against the man who is engaged
in working the greatest damage against him.

—Richard Baxter, seventeenth-century English Puritan
church leader, poet, hymn writer, and theologian

It's starting to smell a little like danger
in here, or heavily fried food.

—The Tick, animated superhero

I have a cherished live recording of gospel legend Mavis Staples
performing at the fiftieth anniversary celebration of the Newport
Folk Festival in 2009. Mavis and her sisters, under the firm tutelage
of their father, "Pops," had already won fame as The Staple Singers
when they met Martin Luther King Jr. for the first time in 1960, in
the Montgomery, Alabama, church where the great civil rights leader
was preaching. Midway through her Newport performance, Mavis
tells the story of how she and her sisters and father were swept into

the civil rights movement after her father emerged from a private conversation with Dr. King and proclaimed to his daughters: "If he can preach it, we can sing it." From that moment, The Staple Singers were a fixture at Dr. King's rallies, performing songs written by Pops especially for each occasion. But one song—"Why Am I Treated So Bad?"—was a favorite of Dr. King's. Mavis describes the song's backstory at her Newport performance:

> You know, we would sing before Dr. King would speak. And every time we'd get ready to go to a meeting, he would tell Pops, he said, "Now, now, Stape, you're gonna sing my song tonight, right?" Pops said, "Oh yeah … we're gonna sing your song."
>
> (Now singing) "Why … am I treated so bad? Tell me … why am I treated so bad? You know I'm all alone as I sing this song. Hear my call, I done nobody wrong. But I'm treated so bad…. That's all right. That's all right. You can't harm me. You can't harm me. I got the Lord on my side. Yes! I'm gonna walk out in the Master's name. Things I do, everything I do, they seem to be in vain. You may be blind, you may be lame. Walk on out in the Master's name, though you're treated so bad. That's all you gotta do. Well, it's a mighty long lane. You know it got no end. It's a bad wind, you know don't ever change. Listen, I think I heard somebody call my name, saying further up the road things are

going to change. Still, I'm treated so bad. Still, I'm
treated so bad....

(Now explaining) You know, my grandma, she
was a wise lady. My grandma would walk around
the house all day long, just moaning. Yeah, she
would moan, y'all. My grandma, she would moan
while she was cookin'. She would moan while she
was working in her garden. And she would moan
while making her handmade quilts, you know?
And I didn't understand this moaning. I like to
sing, but I never did moan. So, I would follow
her around the house all day—I was just a little
girl, you know—listening to Grandma moan. So
I decided, I'm gonna find out what this moaning is
about. One day I got up enough nerve to ask her.
I said, "Grandma, why do you moan like that all
the time?" She said, "Well, baby, when you moan,
the Devil don't know what you're talking about."
So sometimes when I get so weary ... *(Now singing)*
I get tired, I get tired, I get tired of being talked
about. I get tired of being called out by names, I
get tired of being abused. I get so tired, y'all. And
I think about my grandma, I fold my arms, and I
begin to moan. Oooh, oooh, oooh. I don't want
him in my business, either. No, I don't want him to
know what I'm talking about. Oooh, oooh, oooh.
Oh yeah—my, my. You may be blind, you may be
lame, walk on out in the Master's name. Though

you're treated so bad, although you're treated so
bad, though you're treated so bad, treated so bad.[1]

Yes, just like Grandma Staples, we expect the Devil to "treat us so bad." And why wouldn't we moan our prayers instead of speak them, if there's any chance the Devil is listening to them? In the message of this song—and in Grandma Staples' mysterious behavior—is a self-evident truth so commonly accepted that it's become like wallpaper in our souls. It's a background truth that we just don't think about anymore because it's as fundamental to us as breathing. And it is this:

We intrinsically abhor the person and work of Satan in our lives.

Grandma Staples moaned because she was operating out of a basic distrust of God's Enemy—she didn't want him to "know her business" because he would, she was sure, use it against her. Only psychopaths or people who are ignorant of Satan's true activities revere him. Far from acting as his confidantes and coconspirators, we wrestle against demonic influence in our lives and grieve over its destructive impact—"I'm treated so bad." We would never consciously give God's Enemy ground in our lives because we know that he "kills, steals, and destroys."[2] Even people who don't follow Christ also refuse to follow Satan because we're hardwired to be repulsed by his fundamental nature. Even more, saints like Grandma Staples feel such a visceral disgust and distrust for Satan that they protect their tender places from him—guarding their conversations with God, moaning rather than risking exposure and, therefore, fueling their Enemy's schemes.

And even though these truths are self-evident, they are in *stark contrast* to the Enemy's expectations when he first infected the loyalties of Adam and Eve, then suggested their casual betrayal, then deflowered their innocence. His was a naked assumption: that he'd just gained two powerful new allies in his ongoing war against heaven. Now that they had "the knowledge of good and evil," he reasoned, insurrection would look as good to them as it did to him. After all, the fundamental temptation he'd insinuated into Adam and Eve's idyllic life was that they could "be like gods," and that God knew it and was holding out on them. This is the same lie he told himself to justify his betrayal of the One who created him and loved him.

So, in his temptation of Adam and Eve, Satan also reveals the way he thinks. He already considers himself a god—essentially a rival gang leader who's amassing his own guerilla army to overthrow what amounts to a rival of equal standing. In John's fantastical vision of the cataclysmic events that preceded the fall, in the book of Revelation, we learn that Lucifer succeeded in convincing one-third of all heaven's angels to join him in his insurrection (Rev. 12). Not a bad ratio if your goal is to turn God's beloved against Him. So imagine Lucifer's shock when, in the first of many outflanking maneuvers launched by the Trinity, the fallen First Couple and all their progeny instead become his *fundamental enemies*.

In an 1876 sermon delivered by Charles H. Spurgeon, the great English preacher tracks our embedded repulsion for Satan back to its source:

> He who is born into this world but once, and knows
> nothing of the new birth, must place himself among
> the seed of the serpent, for only by regeneration can

we know ourselves to be the true seed. How does God deal with us who are his called and chosen ones? He means to save us, and how does he work to that end?

The first thing he does is, he comes to us in mercy, and *puts enmity between us and the serpent* [Gen. 3:15]. That is the very first work of grace. There was peace between us and Satan once; when he tempted we yielded; whatever he taught us we believed; we were his willing slaves. But perhaps you, my brethren, can recollect when first of all you began to feel uneasy and dissatisfied; the world's pleasures no longer pleased you; all the juice seemed to have been taken out of the apple, and you had nothing at all. Then you suddenly perceived you were living in sin, and you were miserable about it, and though you could not get rid of sin yet you hated it, and sighed over it, and cried, and groaned. In your heart of hearts you remained no longer on the side of evil, for you began to cry [in the apostle Paul's words], "O wretched man that I am, who shall deliver me from the body of this death?"[3]

Yes, we are at enmity with Satan and his legions … thank God.

And that is precisely why any "productive" dialogue between God and Satan is so shocking and unbelievable to us.

And yet, the fact of it is undeniable. We have an overpowering and comprehensive Old Testament example in Job and a scandalous

New Testament example in Jesus' "sifting" warning to Peter. Jesus is in conversation with Satan, who apparently makes requests, which are seriously considered and either denied or approved. Take away the last two-thirds of this progression and there remains still a disturbing reality: God is regularly in conversation with Satan. The New Testament records twenty-one separate conversations between Jesus and Satan or his demons. Our redeemed repulsion for the character and behavior of Satan makes it almost impossible to believe (or explain) God's decision to permit him entrée into our lives.

Bob Krulish will often surprise people by asking them: "How's your relationship with Satan today?" Bob is the first to admit this question makes a lot of people confused, uncomfortable, and even angry. I was taken off guard the first time he asked me to answer it. But now I find its implication scandalously true—we, like our Master Jesus, *all* have an active relationship with Satan (or more likely, members of his host, since Satan is not able by nature to be in all places at once), whether or not we're aware of it or feel comfortable admitting it. Once, after Bob told me he'd asked a group of men at a morning Bible study his "question," he described their response:

> Surprise and maybe even "indignant" was the immediate "feel" response. But when we consider Jesus has a relationship with Satan [in Luke 22 and elsewhere] and the Trinity as a whole has a relationship with Satan (in Genesis, Job, and elsewhere), it makes pondering the question at least plausible. If I interviewed him, what would he say are his schemes against you—do you even know what they are?

> Why do we ignore our adversary? When I played
> professional basketball we spent one-third of the
> time studying our adversary so we would not be
> caught off guard. The other two-thirds of our time
> we practiced what we did well.[4]

So, okay, maybe we can somehow get our minds around Jesus'
sitting down with Satan at a Starbucks instead of cutting his head
off with a sword, but how could He entertain or, worse, tolerate
the cruel demands of a defeated fallen angel? Why would a God
who says He loves us, who gave up His own Son for our salvation,
consider *any request* from a being whose *only* motivation is vain
hatred and whose *only* activities are focused on our destruction?
Hasn't God promised to stand between us and our Enemy? Didn't
Jesus come to "destroy the works of the Devil"? How can God
possibly violate His own foundational decree of "enmity"?

It's a mystery and a paradox—but not without its clues. My
friend and pastor Tom Melton once told me: "Nothing is paradoxical to God, it's only paradoxical to us. Our own experience as
parents applies here—our kids don't always understand that what
we do is grounded in love, especially when what we do hurts them.
It's a paradox to them, but not to us." And as the iconic literary
figure Sherlock Holmes demonstrates, the truth behind apparent
mysteries—our great paradoxes—remains hidden to us unless we
use a lens, a kind of magnifying glass, to study them more closely.
Holmes lives by a functional motto that the truth is always revealed
in the details. Study closely the details through a clarifying lens
and you will, he vows, unlock their truths. And in this case—the

mystery of God's apparently collusive relationship with Satan—*the lens we need is the one called "God is good."*

In a debate with prominent atheist Christopher Hitchens, the evangelical theologian and pastor Douglas Wilson said: "Everybody who's finite and limited has to have an axiomatic starting point. That axiomatic starting point is your faith position."[5] And in our exploration of what is at least a disturbing reality and at most an apparent betrayal, we'll choose "God is good" as our "axiomatic starting point," the lens we choose to get at the truth. "Good" is how the Bible and (more specifically) Jesus' own words describe His fundamental nature, over and over. So we will take our cue from the woman who responded to *Smith Magazine*'s "six-word memoir" challenge[6] by condensing her life story into this: "I spell God with two o's." We will make a fundamental assumption that God is good, then travel from there. Sherlock Holmes, voicing Sir Arthur Conan Doyle, offers us this guiding advice: "When you have excluded the impossible, whatever remains, however improbable, must be the truth."[7] It is, of course, an improbable conclusion that God is good when He gives Satan permission to sift His beloved, but the alternatives are, in the end, impossible.

Satan's Sense and Sensibility

The other day I heard a young pastor say something that sounded bold and fierce and true and therefore Jesus-like. But my soul reacted as if it had sniffed poison. Here is what the pastor said:

"Maybe there is a way for us to become so dangerous that the darkness doesn't want anything to do with us."

The obvious flaw is that no one has ever been more dangerous than Jesus, and Satan certainly stalked Him like a shark sensing blood in the water. And all of Jesus' disciples, except for John, died a violent, horrific death. And Hebrews 11 catalogs the horrible things done to the faithful believers who are our "cloud of witnesses." Spurgeon recalibrates with this: "The devil is the greatest of all fools. He has more knowledge but less wisdom than any other creature, he is more subtle than all the beasts of the field, but it is well called *subtlety*, not wisdom."[8] The poison in the pastor's challenge emanates from a mix of youthful bravado and a profound inattentiveness to the character and motivation of God's Enemy. Again, as Bob Krulish reminds us, ignorance of our adversary invites him to exercise a kind of "competitive leverage"—but we are redeemed and rescued by God solely because He has *never* surrendered competitive leverage to His Enemy. He is well aware of His adversary's character and motivation, and is not at all surprised by his schemes. And because Satan is a foolish foe he's not that hard to expose—a closer scrutiny of his words and actions through the lens of "God is good" strips away the veneer that keeps us from understanding his true nature.

1. Satan does not operate out of legitimate legal authority; he navigates solely by deceptive and illegitimate legal authority.

I have a young friend who's been a professional illusionist since he was seven years old—he's now eighteen. Sometimes, after a show, someone will casually refer to him as a "magician," but he quickly corrects the mistake—he uses *illusion*, not magic (he insists), to do what looks impossible. Magic would imply access to darker powers, and he wants those astounded by what they've seen to know he's merely tricking them. By definition a magician may have supernatural power, but an illusionist merely fools our senses into believing a lie. And, of course, Satan is also a professional illusionist—he has no real legal power or authority of his own, so he must steal ours by deceiving us. He is the original identity thief. Tom Melton observes: "For Satan to demand anything from God is comical—he's the Wizard of Oz pulling levers behind a curtain. He's imposing and scary right up to the moment a little dog pulls the curtain away and exposes him for the poser he is."[9]

Therapist and pastor David Hay, a student of demonic motivation and behavior, points out that God always moves within the legal boundaries He's set up—He makes and keeps covenants with His people and even His enemies. After the "war in heaven" (Rev. 12:7–9), when God emerges victorious over Satan and his insurrectionist army of rebel angels, the defeated foes are spared destruction and, instead, cast down to earth where they are given a measure of legal authority to rule. In fact, prior to His death and resurrection, Jesus calls His adversary "the ruler of this world." Hay points to the Old Testament for evidence of God's legal maneuvering, where He moves through history, making covenant after covenant with His chosen people—all of it essentially legal positioning to prepare the way for the birth, life, death, and resurrection of Jesus. Only the spotless sacrifice of His Son, the "second Adam," would finally redeem the betrayal of the first Adam. The Old Testament sometimes reads like a chess match between two lawyers, but there are plenty of New Testament examples of God's "legal" strategy to take back what Adam and Eve gave away—for example, Galatians 4:4–7:

> When the fullness of the time came, God sent forth
> His Son, born of a woman, born under the Law, so

that He might redeem those who were under the
Law, that we might receive the adoption as sons.
Because you are sons, God has sent forth the Spirit
of His Son into our hearts, crying, "Abba! Father!"
Therefore you are no longer a slave, but a son; and
if a son, then an heir through God.

So when Jesus arrives in enemy territory—"born of a woman,
born under the Law"—He quickly asserts His legal authority over
the "prince of the power of the air" and his corrupted angels. Hay
insists: "Jesus came expressly to assert His authority and 'destroy the
works of the devil.' He didn't bargain with demonic forces, He just
cast them out. He told everyone who would listen that 'the kingdom
of God is near'—He meant that the authority structure on earth
was now upended by His presence. 'If you see Me, you've seen the
Father.'"[10]

The Bible tells us that, in the three days between His crucifixion and His resurrection, Jesus descended into the bottom of hell,
where He simply took back the nominal legal authority granted to
Satan after the fall of Adam and Eve. And then, as He repeatedly
told His disciples in the days after His resurrection and before His
ascension, Jesus transferred that legal authority to His followers:
"All authority has been given to Me in heaven and on earth. Go
therefore and make disciples of all the nations, baptizing them in
the name of the Father and the Son and the Holy Spirit" (Matt.
28:18–19). The "therefore" connotes a handoff of the baton.
Imagine the gravelly voice of John Wayne asserting, "Pilgrim,
there's a new sheriff in town."

Perhaps because of His mercy, but more likely because of His own redemptive purposes, Jesus leaves Satan and his demons on the earth, but their legal authority is no longer in effect. They are now lonely, disembodied spirits. This is exactly why Jesus can advise us, matter-of-factly: "Resist the devil and he will flee from you" (James 4:7). Satan is, essentially, a lawyer who operates shrewdly under the constraints of legal authority. Since all legal authority has been stripped from him, his strategies and schemes depend upon deception and subterfuge as he attempts to entice us into handing over to him our own legal authority won for us by Jesus' death and resurrection. In his essence Satan is an authority-sucking leech who is wholly dependent on his "host" for permission to live and breathe and move. When we consciously or unconsciously offer up our authority to him—allowing him to use it as a proxy in his war against God's beloved—we become his functional allies. If we only understood how precarious this arrangement is, we would be far less impressed with Satan and far less likely to let him leech off of us. David Hay offers an example of this simple exercise of authority in the story of a client who was referred to him by a local hospital after the man complained of hearing voices that were driving him crazy:

> He was acting out at work, he was out of charac-
> ter, screaming at his wife and daughter. They had
> paranormal experiences in their house. His wife was
> scared and threatened to take their daughter and go
> back to their country of origin. So the whole family
> decided to return to their original country, where
> they sought out a mystic to get relief from all the

paranormal activity. As a result a demonic presence, using the voice of the mystic, entered into the man. The voice would not stop harassing him. I had compassion for this man, so when we met I asked to speak to the demon. I asked for and discovered he had a name, and I addressed him by that name. He was kind of bargaining with me. But I told the demon to go back to the Lord Jesus and report into Him. For a couple of minutes he argued, but then the man looked up at me and said, "He's gone." I saw him this week—there are still no voices. When we engage a demon we're in total authority.[11]

Acts 19 records the incredible story of a group of Jewish exorcists who were traveling from town to town in the vicinity of Ephesus, casting out demons. They'd heard about the apostle Paul and all the incredible miracles that followed in his wake, so they decided to start using the name of Jesus as a sort of incantation in their exorcisms, just to see if they could add it to their repertoire. But things go badly for them: "One time when they tried it, the evil spirit replied, 'I know Jesus, and I know Paul, but who are you?' Then the man with the evil spirit leaped on them, overpowered them, and attacked them with such violence that they fled from the house, naked and battered" (vv. 15–16 NLT).

It's the *authority* of Jesus, not His name used as an incantation, that functions like a tsunami washing over the forces of darkness. "I know Jesus, and I know Paul. But who are you?"—it's a one-two-punch theological treatise on the way things are....

So, without any authority to operate independently, the enemies of God are reduced to deception, illusion, and trickery. That is why another of Satan's names is "the Tempter." When we sin we unwittingly open ourselves to demonic influence not because Satan's decommissioned mob has the authority to harass us, but expressly because our shame makes us reluctant to move in the authority Christ won for those who follow Him. It's true that his loss of legal authority seems to have impacted Lucifer's fundamental arrogance not at all. Satan loves his own beauty—that's what motivated him to challenge God's authority in the first place. In Ezekiel 28:17 God describes Lucifer's expulsion from heaven this way: "Your heart became proud on account of your beauty, and you corrupted your wisdom because of your splendor. So I threw you to the earth; I made a spectacle of you before kings" (NIV).

Satan wasn't satisfied with his "place"—enticed by his own opinion of himself, further fueled by those future rebel angels who were intoxicated by his beauty, he wanted more. In this way he's like Absalom, David's son, who schemed to usurp his father's power first through negotiation, then through outright rebellion aimed at not only dethroning his father, but killing him. There are even hints of Satan's story in the parable of the prodigal son—the younger brother in the story also ends up as an outcast outside his father's kingdom ... but was welcomed back because he repented. What if the Prodigal had responded with rage and retribution instead of repentance? He would, of course, have been the passionate enemy of his father, blaming him for all his woes and defending the "beauty" of his rebellion.

Dare 2 Share founder Greg Stier says: "Satan is not a fatalist—he does not easily give in to 'the facts on the ground.' He retains his intelligence, but he's growing more and more insane, like Hitler toward the end of his life."[12] That insanity is on display in Satan's encounter with Jesus, when he demands (the Greek word is *exaiteo*, which means "to ask for with emphasis and with implication of having a right to do so") the permission to "sift" Peter and the disciples. Embedded in the request is an oxymoron—the "demand" comes from someone who's reduced to asking permission. But keep in mind that Jesus has not yet suffered and died on the cross and wrested back Satan's legal privileges in hell—Satan still operates with a measure of authority, but not before the throne of God. There, he brings nothing to the table but the kind of obsessive vendetta that fueled the character Salieri in the film *Amadeus*. In a pivotal scene Salieri, Austria's royal court composer, hurls a crucifix into his chamber fireplace. He's furious because God has gifted Mozart—the boyish and often crude composer who is his rival—with a genius for creating "the music of the gods." Rather than embrace and enable Mozart's gift, Salieri vows to "ruin [God's] incarnation."[13] His envy twists him into a murderer—an enemy of God who subjugates all that he is to a single purpose: destroying Mozart as an act of revenge against a capricious God. Something very like this is described in Revelation 12:13: "When the dragon saw that he had been hurled to the earth, he pursued the woman who had given birth to the male child" (NIV).

This is why Satan has the audacity to ask Jesus for clearance to "sift" Peter. His strategy is built on assumptions he holds so deeply that it's literally impossible for him to take in new information. Stier adds: "Satan is before the throne all the time asking for permission slips. In Jacob's dream [Genesis 28:10–16], angels are going up and down the ladder to heaven—it's a dream, but it's a metaphor for Satan gaining access to the Father. His motivation is envy—described in great detail in Ezekiel 28 and Isaiah 14—he's convinced he can overcome God. He's so self-deceived with his own strength and beauty that he believes he's going to win in the end, because there was a point where he thought he could take Jesus out. And he doesn't think any differently now."[14]

2. Satan is detailed, organized, shrewd, and systems-oriented.

In my senior year at college I volunteered to be the official photographer for an elite women's choir that was going to Poland for a two-week tour. The reason, of course, was selfish: The girl I was dating/stalking (who is now, miraculously, my wife) was in this choir, and I had romantic visions of the two of us traveling Europe together, sipping espresso and making wry comments about architecture. It was, to say the least, a disaster on the romantic front—she spent a good amount of her time on the trip flirting with exotic European young men, excitedly pronouncing their names to me with European accuracy. Oh, and even though I'd trained in photography as part of my journalism schooling, most of the flashless photographs I took turned out so dark they might as well have been Rorschach blotches. It was a miserable two weeks.

Midway through the trip, we got on our bus for a trek across the barren Polish landscape to Auschwitz, where the choir was scheduled to sing a series of beautiful laments in the shadow of the ovens where hundreds of thousands of Jews were incinerated after they'd been gassed in what they were told were "showers." I'll never forget that day—as the bus pulled up to the gates of the concentration camp the giddy laughter and buzzing conversation that was our constant backdrop inside the bus muted, as if someone had pushed a button. The understood quiet lasted all day. The original gates still stood, with the mocking words "Work Brings Freedom" formed out of iron, insinuating to new arrivals that the purpose of the camp was to confine them while they performed necessary labor for the Third Reich. In fact, once their train passed through those gates and stopped to unload its exhausted human cargo, the people climbing out of their cattle cars would see that the tracks ended inside the camp. Most were dead before nightfall.

Polish officials turned one of the surviving barracks into a kind of museum to help visitors understand what had happened there. On one end was a massive floor-to-ceiling glass encasement that held what was left of the human hair the Nazis had "harvested" before sending their victims to the "showers"—the gas houses. On the other end was a massive floor-to-ceiling glass encasement for the leftover luggage of victims who'd carefully marked each piece with their names and addresses so they could retrieve their personal items at the camp—instead, their luggage was simply tossed into a pile, where Nazi officials would later sift for valuables. In between were several informational displays that explained the meticulous and detailed system the Nazis had set up to record every torturous act of "medical experimentation," every ounce of gold pried from victims' teeth, and every material possession that was valuable enough to save. We know exactly what happened in that camp because the Nazis were obsessively organized mass murderers. They had a plan and procedure for the most horrific of human acts—it's the sign of a collective insanity, and the imprint of Satan's very personality.

Efficiency, organization, and copious attention to detail are always embedded in his "work." That's why three of his names include the word "ruler."

In Ephesians 6:12 Paul describes what this systemic approach to evil looks like: "For our struggle is not against flesh and blood, but against the rulers, against the powers, against the world forces of this darkness, against the spiritual forces of wickedness in the heavenly places." In Daniel 10 the angel Gabriel appears to the prophet and explains why his visit was so delayed: "Do not be afraid, Daniel, for from the first day that you set your heart on understanding this and on humbling yourself before your God, your words were heard, and I have come in response to your words. But the prince of the kingdom of Persia was withstanding me for twenty-one days; then behold, Michael, one of the chief princes, came to help me, for I had been left there with the kings of Persia" (vv. 12–13). So, in effect, a fallen angel whose jurisdiction was Persia is deployed by Satan to stop the angel Gabriel from delivering an important message to Daniel. God has to send his own "enforcer"—Michael the archangel—to remove the "obstacle." We get only peeks into the "Nazi apparatus" that wages war on God and His children, but what we see is disciplined, organized, and methodical.

Satan pays obsessive attention to details, but not in the personal way that God does. Tom Melton says: "God knows the number of hairs on everyone's head. But Satan would not take the time to know your name. He would never call you by name because he's very impersonal. His operation is to destroy, and he does it by dehumanizing."[15] Spurgeon weighs in: "We doubt not that [Satan] views the Lord's people, and especially the more eminent and excellent among them, as the great barriers to the progress of his kingdom; and just as the engineer, endeavoring to make a railway, keeps his eye very much fixed upon the hills and rivers, and especially upon the great mountain through which it will take years laboriously to bore a tunnel, so Satan, in looking upon his various plans to carry on his dominion in the world, considers most such men [who stand in his way]."[16]

Just as an engineer studies the obstacles in the way of his project before developing a systematic plan for overcoming them, the forces of darkness study and similarly brand us "obstacles," not people. The other day at the health club I belong to, my spinning instructor was fuming about something that he'd seen the previous day. He was working out in the weight room when a guy noticed the blinds were down on the side of the room that looks out on a beautiful garden. So he started to raise the blinds so the people working out could see the bed of tulips bursting up through the ground a few feet away. But a man called out from across the weight room—"Don't raise that blind!" The other man, startled, stopped what he was doing, paused, then let the blind down again. The man who'd called out added, as if it was an afterthought—but loudly enough for everyone in the weight room to hear: "I'm planning to cut a bunch of those tulips and take them home." A few people nervously laughed. And then, a little while later, the "tulip cutter" finished his workout and left.

Some minutes after that, the man who'd earlier started to raise the blind noticed the tulip cutter was gone, so he went over to pull up the blind again. Like the curtain going up on a play, the raised blind revealed a shocking scene—the tulip cutter was standing in the garden with a pair of scissors, cutting off the last of the flowers and adding it to the huge bunch in his hand. He paid no attention to the people in the weight room. With his decapitations complete, he turned on his heel for the parking lot. The people watching inside the club froze, stunned by the man's indifferent brutality—he wanted the tulips, so he cut them off and took them home. He cared nothing, *nothing*, about robbing others in the health club of that beauty. The people working out next to him were essentially inanimate objects— as much a part of the landscape as those tulips, and just as likely to be cut down if that's what would be useful. They merely represented a thwarting obstacle to his narcissism.

The tulip cutter's thought processes are not only satanic but exactly in line with the collective mind-set of the Nazis, who obliterated the moral ramparts that protected the German state, mass-murdering six million Jews as if they were crabgrass. Satan "kills and steals and destroys" the same way you or I pull weeds. Spurgeon drives home the point: "Satan watches and considers first of all our peculiar infirmities. He looks us up and down, just as I have seen a horse-dealer do with a horse; and soon finds out wherein we are faulty. I, a common observer, might think the horse an exceedingly good one, as I see it running up and down the road, but the dealer sees what I cannot see, and he knows how to handle the creature."[17]

So, when Satan approaches the Trinity to ask for permission to sift Peter and the disciples—and, by extension, anyone else who stands in his way—he is intending to leverage what he has discovered about the "obstacle" in his way and either destroy it or turn it to himself. It's not personal, just as it wasn't personal for the Nazis during World War II—they were highly impersonal and efficient "removers of obstacles."

3. Satan has no ability to understand the heart of man or, even more, the heart of God.

Because Lucifer is a betrayer at his core, deception is central to his identity—it is not a behavior but his *essence*. In John 8 Jesus describes him: "He was a murderer from the beginning, and does not stand in the truth because there is no truth in him. Whenever he speaks a lie, he speaks from his own nature, for he is a liar and the father of lies" (v. 44). A being whose very nature is to lie and betray will also assume that all others—even the God who created him—have a similar nature. Satan hates God not because he hates goodness, but because he believes he's been outsmarted and outflanked by a being—in his mind, very like himself—who has used the tools of deceit and betrayal better than he has. God, in the Enemy's belief system, has even managed to deceive the rabble humans that He is good and that He loves them. Salieri despises Mozart because he is a base human being; he hates him because he's managed to gain the respect of the world because of a gift haphazardly bestowed. Satan, likewise, continues to approach God with demands and schemes because he believes God's heart is fatally flawed like his own, and it's only a matter of time before he can find the "crack" in God's armor that he's confident is there.

We see evidence of this belief system in the voice of an "unclean spirit" in Luke 4 who barks at Jesus: "Let us alone! What business do we have with each other, Jesus of Nazareth? Have You come to destroy us? I know who You are—the Holy One of God!" (v. 34). The spirit assumes Jesus is there to destroy him, and the evidence it has for that twisted belief is its supposed understanding of His heart—"I know who you are." But he doesn't know who Jesus is, not even a little. The Master tells the spirit to be quiet and commands him to come out of the man he is oppressing. That's it. Mercy, not destruction.

Spurgeon, in a sermon delivered in 1865 at the Metropolitan Tabernacle in Newington, says:

> The consideration which Satan pays to God's saints is upon this wise. *He regards them with wonder, when he considers the difference between them and himself.* A traitor, when he knows the thorough villainy and the blackness of his own heart, cannot help being astounded, when he is forced to believe another man to be faithful. The first resort of a treacherous heart is to believe that all men would be just as treacherous, and are really so at bottom. The traitor thinks that all men are traitors like himself, or would be, if it paid them better than fidelity. When Satan looks at the Christian, and finds him faithful to God and to his truth, he considers him as we should consider a phenomenon—perhaps despising him for his folly, but yet marveling at him, and wondering how he can act thus.[18]

And so Satan is convinced that if he's allowed to "sift" Peter and the disciples the process will expose the darkness of their hearts—that their seeming devotion to Jesus will give way to the same kind of cowardly, self-obsessed, greedy, and traitorous essence that he knows so well in his own being. He is confident, as he was with Job, that

Peter will show his true colors once he puts the screws to him: "Does Job fear God for nothing? Have You not made a hedge about him and his house and all that he has, on every side? You have blessed the work of his hands, and his possessions have increased in the land. But put forth Your hand now and touch all that he has; he will surely curse You to Your face" (Job 1:9–11). Here Satan exposes his deeply held beliefs about all human beings—and he lives it out again centuries later with Peter. And, just as the early results of Satan's plot to murder God's Son seem successful, Peter seems to reward Satan's "he will surely curse you" assumption by cracking under the weight of his sifting. It is an absolute shock to the Evil One that Jesus rises from the dead and that Peter later returns to lead the church.

God's Sense and Sensibility

Between "Simon, Simon, Satan has asked …" and "but I have prayed for you …" is a chasm of understanding that seems too wide for us to cross. Satan asks, and Jesus gives His permission. Blood, sweat, and tears fill up that lonely chasm. What happens to Peter is heartbreaking, no matter what follows.

The thing that has always bothered me about the way we typically read the Bible is how obviously distant we are from these epic stories. At a small gathering of friends, author and philosophy professor Dallas Willard said: "One of the bad things that's happened in the church is that people don't read Paul or Jesus as if what they've said has real application to our lives."[19] So true.

I loved reading Hardy Boys mysteries when I was a boy, but I never considered that Chet would skid up to my house in his jalopy with Frank and Joe hanging on in the backseat, then knock on my door to ask if I needed help solving "The Mystery of the Disappearing Socks." These are mere stories, after all. And however much we blur the boundary between fiction and nonfiction, most of us approach stories as outside observers—we are not *in* the story, and therefore the story is not *in* us. This dynamic ruins most Bible stories for us.

In Mark Galli's book *Jesus Mean and Wild,* he describes a tipping-point moment when his own distant relationship to the stories of the Bible was exposed. Galli was pastor of a California church when a group of Laotian refugees asked if they could become members. He offered to lead them through a study of Mark's gospel as a foundational exercise before they made their commitment. The Laotians had little knowledge of Scripture or of Jesus. When Galli got to the passage where Jesus calms the storm, he asked the refugees to talk about the "storms" in their lives—their problems, worries, and struggles. The people looked confused and puzzled. Galli filled the awkward silence by asking again, "So what are your storms?" Finally, one of the Laotian men asked, "Do you mean that Jesus actually calmed the wind and sea in the middle of a storm?" Galli thought the man was merely expressing his skepticism, and the study really had little to do with an actual exploration of Jesus' miracles, so he said: "Yes, but we should not get hung up on the details of the miracle. We should remember that Jesus can calm the storms in our lives." After another awkward pause, one of the men excitedly proclaimed: "Well, if Jesus calmed the wind and the waves, he must be a very powerful man!" The Laotians erupted in excitement over the incredible authority exhibited by the man Galli described in Scripture. Galli, meanwhile, looked on the celebration as a virtual outsider. While these newbie Christian refugees got caught up into a kind of naked worship, Galli felt locked out of the Holy of Holies because he'd never really treated the story as *real*.[20]

This is exactly why we read the book of Job as a kind of moralistic fairy tale with a happy ending—the man gains back his riches and soon has a new family to "replace" the one he lost. But we miss the aching sorrow and grief he must have felt for those he loved who are now gone, and for the innocence he's lost forever. And we're too quick to move past the impact of Peter's sifting—the long, sleepless nights of grief and self-recrimination and weeping and (perhaps) the suicidal thoughts that his former brother Judas carried to completion. Satan's requests, and God's permissions, have price tags attached to them that seem entirely too high for us to accept. Satan's demands are horrific; God's apparent acquiescence to these demands is beyond offensive.

As I prepared to write this book, my church asked me to fill in for Tom Melton and preach about "sifted like wheat." I felt both excitement and dread. Excitement, because there is a truth in this encounter that touches the deepest places in our souls and reveals the deepest places in God's good heart. Dread, because I knew I'd be looking out on the faces of people who are slowly dying from terminal diseases, devastated because of divorce, frightened to the point of panic because of financial collapse, haunted by the violence and disrespect that are common in their homes, furious because of the sexual abuse they experienced many years ago, and grieving over children who are self-destructing. And five rows back, just behind the area where my wife and girls will be sitting, will be a mother and father who've been told by doctors that their little girl has only months to live. She plays soccer with my daughter. And the parents haven't told her yet because they can't bear to do it. And there she is, sitting with them in church with a big smile on her face while her mom fights to hold it together for one more hour.

How can I possibly tell them, and all the other faces that mask private holocausts, that Satan sometimes asks to sift, and Jesus sometimes gives His permission?

I know this: Real life requires more than rhetorical truisms, religious equations, and jargon-y metaphors—and this is precisely the territory where we get hopelessly lost without our magnifying lens, which is, "God is good."

1. God is never leveraged by evil.

Yes, God is in conversation with Lucifer. More than that, He listens patiently and respectfully to his requests—we know this because Jesus tells us that He is the perfect mirror image of the God we can't see ("He who has seen Me has seen the Father" [John 14:9]), and He is patient and respectful in the presence of Satan and his demons. Because God is secure in His own goodness, there is no reason for Him to fear or dread engaging one whose very nature is in opposition to His own. This is one of the many examples of how God's ways are not our ways (Isa. 55:8)—we have very little patience for the opinions and diatribes of those who spout views diametrically opposed to our own because we're typically afraid of the leverage those views can have on us.

A tipping point in my own life with God happened when I began listening to talk radio almost twenty years ago. Until then, I'd avoided the medium the same way I avoid torture and asparagus. I literally couldn't bear to listen to the impassioned arguments of people whose beliefs were radically different from my own—I felt threatened and violated by their worldviews and by their anchoring perspectives. One day, as I was making the long commute to work, I felt compelled to counteract my cowardice by tuning my radio to a local talk show that had been perpetually intolerable to me. I pushed the button, then braced myself like a man preparing to stand in the face of a crashing wave. I can endure it for five minutes today, I told myself. The next day it was ten, and I finally worked my way up to a full half hour by the end of the week. Gradually, my soul began to relax in the torrent of words, just the way my body began to relax as I was learning how to ride a bike as a kid—that week I oodged my way toward a trusting reliance on my emerging sense of balance. Yes, I could handle the impassioned arguments of those who are profoundly lost without it toppling my foundation.

The fear I'd harbored toward the onslaughts of talk radio was the direct by-product of my deep belief that contrary arguments could easily sway me. I'm redeemed, but not perfected. And that means I, like you, have feet of clay. My sins—or even my memory of them—are the fulcrum Satan uses to leverage his purposes in me. But Jesus feels no such fear because He has no sin fulcrum to leverage. At the start of His ministry on earth, Jesus was "led up by the Spirit into the wilderness to be tempted by the devil" (Matt. 4:1). So, as casually as you or I might arrange to have coffee with a friend, the third person of the Trinity arranges a tête-à-tête with Lucifer for the second person of the Trinity. And Satan takes his best swing at a hungry and depleted Jesus—tempting Him not once, but three times, and even quoting Scripture to back up his challenge to jump from the pinnacle of the temple. Though He has the authority to do it, Jesus won't send His Enemy away after his first outrageous assault, nor the second. Only when Jesus has determined that the Trinity's subversive purpose in allowing Satan's temptations has been accomplished does He command, "Away with you!" All the control in this scene is in Jesus' hands—He plays His Enemy like a saxophone, allowing his temptations only because they serve His strategic mission on earth ("Because he himself suffered when he was tempted, he is able to help those who are being tempted" [Heb. 2:18 NIV]). Jesus is relaxed, never threatened by the plausible lies thrown at Him.

In His sprawling attempt to reassure His confused and frightened disciples as His pace to the cross quickens (John 14) Jesus reveals to us the reason for His relaxed stance toward the Enemy's attempts to leverage Him: "For the ruler of the world is coming, and he has nothing in Me" (v. 30). You might call "nothing in Me" the language of engineers—it references the physics of leverage. Architect, illustrator, and author David Macaulay, in *The Way Things Work*, describes a lever as "simply a bar or rod that tilts on a pivot, or fulcrum. If you apply a force by pushing or pulling on one part of the lever, the lever swings about the fulcrum to produce a useful action at another point. The force that you apply is called the *effort*, and the lever moves at another point to raise a weight or overcome a resistance, both of which are called the *load*."[21] Because Satan believes God's heart is as flawed as his own, he spends all his *efforts* attempting to move the *load* of God's love for His creation by experimenting with one lever after another.

But he can't find a fulcrum in God's perfect goodness, and thus his efforts are exposed as the ridiculous imaginations of a delusional despot. God, for His part, is free to simply redirect Satan's attempts at leverage for His own purposes. "Satan has demanded" is merely Jesus' patient revealing of His Enemy's attempt to leverage something in the Trinity and the Trinity's careful consideration of how they might use the mechanics of that attempt to "destroy the works of the devil."[22]

2. There is never a moment when God is not telling the truth.

"Brace for impact." Those were the only words spoken by U.S. Airways pilot Chesley Sullenberger just before he landed his Airbus A320 passenger jet on the Hudson River in 2009, saving all 155 on board after a flock of geese destroyed both engines. He did not say, "It's all going to be okay, don't worry," or, "We're having a little mechanical problem here, but we're working on it." Instead, he told them the plane was about to crash-land on the surface of an urban river, and they should ready themselves for the trauma about to happen. Tom Melton says: "Jesus shared Satan's demand with Peter because He wanted to show him that He could trust him. He tells it like it is."[23] Trust is the currency we spend and receive in all our relationships—if there is no trust, there is no intimacy. And intimacy with His creation is God's chief aim. He cannot nurture intimacy without telling us the truth about the way things are. He is not "sensitive" in the way that we've bastardized the word—as a pandering, disrespectful, and ultimately cheapened replacement for love. In his song "Let Us Down Easy," singer/songwriter Ryan Adams begs:

> *Some of us are strong*
> *But the rest of us are weak*
> *So let us down if you must*
> *But let us down easy, Lord*[24]

Of course, God "knows our frame" and is sensitive to our limita-
tions ("God is faithful; he will not let you be tempted beyond what
you can bear" [1 Cor. 10:13 NIV]). And those who approach Jesus
in brokenness or need most often find in Him a kind of life-giving
sensitivity (the woman caught in adultery, the woman with an issue
of blood, Zacchaeus, and the centurion in Matthew 8, just to name
a few). But He never sacrifices truth on the altar of sensitivity. When
the Canaanite woman in Matthew 15 comes begging for her daughter
to be released from demonic possession, Jesus first tries to brush her
off ("I was sent only to the lost sheep of the house of Israel" [v. 24])
and then bluntly dismisses her: "It is not good to take the children's
bread and throw it to the dogs" (v. 26). This is hardly "letting her
down easy." But the woman rises to the truth bar Jesus has set and
fires back: "'Yes, Lord; but even the dogs feed on the crumbs which
fall from their masters' table.' Then Jesus said to her, 'O woman, your
faith is great; it shall be done for you as you wish.' And her daughter
was healed at once" (v. 27–28).

Jesus never stops telling the truth, and He's not always sensitive
about it. In *Braveheart*, the great Scottish liberator of the thirteenth
century, William Wallace, famously responds to an enemy who
accuses him of being a "bloody murdering savage" and a "liar" by
declaring, in Latin: *"Ego nunquam pronunciari mendacium! Sed ego
sum homo indomitus."* Translated, it means: "I never lie. But I am a

savage." That's a pretty fair description of Jesus, if you understand "savage" to mean "fierce and brave and formidable" in this context. In revealing to Peter Satan's demand, He is investing a kind of blunt respect in him—"Brace yourself for impact." He is telling Peter that something terrible has been schemed about him, and that He is not going to stop it, and that He will be with him.

I remember when I tried out for quarterback on my high school football team—my identity was wrapped up in my ability to throw a football, but my meager athletic gifts could no longer compete head-to-head with big-school talent. The day my coach told me he was switching me to running back (a slow-footed quarterback playing running back?), I came home and told my dad, through my tears, what the coach had said.

"This is just an easy way to get me to quit the team without him having to cut me!" I fumed. "He knows I'll never make it as a running back—don't you think I should quit?"

"Well," my dad replied, "you can certainly quit, and no one would blame you. But just remember that whatever choice you make today will follow you into the rest of your life."

It was a sobering, fierce truth that my soul needed way more than "sensitivity." I chose to stick with the team, getting the stuffing kicked out of me day after day after day. But I earned the respect of that coach, and I found something in my determined heart that I enjoy to this day. That coach told me the truth when he shifted me from quarterback, and my dad told me the truth when he gave me a challenge instead of comfort. God wants nothing to do with cheap imitations of love, and He recognizes (as we most often do not) that there are far worse things that can happen to us than the pain we fear so deeply.

William Paul Young, author of *The Shack*, was asked by a LifeTree Café interviewer: What is God's role in suffering? Young responded:

> [The question is,] how can there be a good God who has the power to stop evil and doesn't[?] [T]here [are] a lot of ways to come at that question. One of the ways that has helped me the most is to realize that God respects His creation way more than we do, that God doesn't just step in and say, "I'm sorry, you've crossed the line, you're not allowed to think that, you're not allowed to do that."... God has not promised that He's ... going to stop it, but He'll show up in the middle of it, and there is nothing so dead that He can't grow something out of it. There's nothing so broken that He can't heal it. And there's not anything so lost He can't find it. So, this idea of His respect for the creation is a little bit of a shock to us because ... we want God to mete ... out [justice for us].... The question is, at what point does He stop our ability to choose evil? ... [T]o love, you have to have the ability to choose. And at what point does He just stop that? He can't, if He wants to have relationship—because coerced love is no love at all. And that is the alternative. He could have made a whole creation that thought they were making free choices, but weren't. There's no relationship there either.[25]

God is bounded by nothing but the self-imposed restraints of love for His creation. And, sometimes, love means He will not "let us down easy." Because He "respects His creation" at a level we struggle to comprehend, we botch the way we translate His movement and restraint in our lives. Philip Yancey writes:

> The more I get to know Jesus, the more impressed I am by ... "the miracle of restraint." ... God's terrible insistence on human freedom is so absolute that he granted us the power to live as though he did not exist, to spit in his face, to crucify him.... I believe God insists on such restraint because no pyrotechnic displays of omnipotence will achieve the response he desires. Although power can force obedience, only love can summon a response of love, which is the one thing God wants from us and the reason he created us.[26]

3. God always goes first.

The first principle of leadership is "going first," and Jesus, like a doctor performing surgery on himself, chooses to submit to Satan's demand to sift Him before He begins His ministry. For thirty years Jesus lives as the carpenter's son. His three-year arc of proclaiming the gospel in word and deed seems like the short trajectory of a bottle rocket in comparison. And bookending the start and finish of his preascension ministry is a strategic experience of sifting. On the front end it's His temptation in the wilderness; at the back end it is His betrayal, arrest, trial, scourging, and crucifixion.

Two months before it was released in theaters I saw a rough cut of Mel Gibson's *The Passion of the Christ*. It was, quite simply, one of the most powerful experiences of my adult Christian life. It's normal to avert our eyes when we see an innocent suffer unrelenting brutality. Gibson's act of courage was to keep his eyes wide open to what actually happened to Jesus, then grit his teeth and put it on film.

A few days after I saw the film, someone asked me how long it was. "I have no idea," I replied. "I lost myself in it." Of course, the film is about two hours long, and it seemed like a quarter of that was Jesus' scourging. There are tears in my eyes right now as I remember those images. Late in the film, as He's about to be nailed to the cross, Jesus (played by James Caviezel) looks up and spits out the words, "Father, my heart is ready!"[27] Those words cut the noose from around our necks. His heart was ready because it had been sifted to the point of despair. Yes, One who had never known anything but intimacy with His Father was suddenly abandoned on the cross by every living thing in the universe: "Daddy, Daddy, why have you forsaken Me?" At the very heart of Jesus' sacrifice on our behalf is Lucifer's demand to sift Jesus and the Trinity's permission to do it.

Jesus always goes first.

Embedded within the parable of the prodigal son—an exacting story-metaphor of God's relationship with His children—is the account of a father who is sifted himself by a wayward younger son and a jaded older son. God's own story orbits around the brutal, dismissive rejection of His beloved children, who demand their entitlements and break His heart. There is no brutality that we endure, no matter how base, that God has not endured first. And because He has walked that wilderness path first, He is well equipped to serve as our companion and guide on our own journey through the valley of the shadow of sifting.

4. God is love, and love allows its beloved to taste the delicious fruits of hardship.

Greg Stier says James 1 holds the secrets to God's motivation for assenting to Satan's demands: "Blessed is a man who perseveres under trial" (v. 12). God doesn't tempt, but He does allow us to experience trials because He wants to bless us. Not exactly a dissonance-neutral truth. But these two look-alikes—trials and temptations—exist in stark contrast. Every problem we face is either a trial sent to us by God to strengthen us or a temptation sent to us by the kingdom of Satan to destroy us or the natural and destructive "produce" of a world that is still reeling under the influence of sin. Joseph said to his brothers who intended to destroy him: "You intended to harm me, but God intended it all for good" (Gen. 50:20 NLT). In Philippians 1 the apostle Paul gets a taste of heaven and is sorely tempted to abort his calling for the raptures that await him—2 Corinthians 12:2 says he was "caught up [in] heaven." So God interjects a trial into his life (a "thorn in my flesh" [v. 7]) that He refuses to blunt or remove. Why? Paul himself soon learns that its purpose is to keep him from getting too cocky about what he saw in heaven—to give him the backbone he'd need to fulfill his mission on earth.

During the early part of World War II, when Germany was pummeling England with daily bombing raids and the weary, heart-broken Brits were just trying to hang on, Prime Minister Winston

Churchill traveled to Harrow, his old Middlesex school, to speak to the students in a special assembly. At the time, England was the lone obstacle in Hitler's path to a true "evil empire." Pearl Harbor was still two months away, and the United States had stayed cautiously on the sideline. In his closing remarks to the students, he said these now-famous words: "Surely from this period of ten months, this is the lesson: Never give in. Never give in. Never, never, never, never— in nothing, great or small, large or petty—never give in, except to convictions of honor and good sense. Never yield to force. Never yield to the apparently overwhelming might of the enemy."[28]

Words like these, from a man like Churchill, infused the British with hope and resolve. Without Churchill's determination to persevere, who knows what our reality would be like today? That's why, in my home, we have his words burned into an old piece of barn wood and mounted above the sink in our kitchen—where everyone can see them every day. It's our family motto—"Never, never, never give up." It somehow reminds me of what the considerably less-heroic Woody Allen once said: "Ninety percent of life is just showing up."

Perseverance, for a follower of Christ, is the "produce" of suffering—it's the organic harvest that transforms our souls from a famine to a feast. Paul reminds us in Romans 5: "We also rejoice in our sufferings, because we know that suffering produces perseverance; perseverance, character; and character, hope" (vv. 3–4 NIV). We can't live and breathe and move without hope. Hope is central to the gospel and to our calling as the midwives of redemption. And we, like farmers, grow our crop of hope through our legacy of perseverance. We can get a peek at what this legacy looks like in nine successive entries taken from the great preacher John Wesley's diary:

- Sunday, a.m., May 5—Preached in St. Anne's. Was asked not to come back anymore.
- Sunday, p.m., May 5—Preached in St. John's. Deacons said, "Get out and stay out."
- Sunday, a.m., May 12—Preached in St. Jude's. Can't go back there, either.
- Sunday, p.m., May 12—Preached in St. George's. Kicked out again.
- Sunday, a.m., May 19—Preached in St. Els's. Deacons called special meeting and said I couldn't return.
- Sunday, p.m., May 19—Preached on street. Kicked off street.
- Sunday, a.m., May 26—Preached in meadow. Chased out of meadow as bull was turned [loose] during service.
- Sunday, a.m., June 2—Preached out at the edge of town. Kicked off the highway.
- Sunday, p.m., June 2—Afternoon, preached in a pasture. Ten thousand people came out to hear me.[29]

Eight failures and a transcendent moment.

Historians estimate that more than one hundred thousand people met the Lord through Wesley's ministry. That's a bumper crop of hope, the result of a lifestyle of endured hardship.

So my own stories of sifting, and yours, are really the lifeblood of our perseverance. God's assent to His Enemy's demand to pound

Peter with hardship is like a gardener's commitment to fertilize his crops—he knows that fertilizer is just the sort of poison that will fundamentally perpetuate his plants' survival in the face of killing assaults. Only an ignorant farmer refuses to fertilize. And only a disrespectful and pandering God keeps His children from the hardships that will make them impervious to the only true fear: "Do not fear those who kill the body but are unable to kill the soul; but rather fear Him who is able to destroy both soul and body in hell" (Matt. 10:28). If the only fear worth having is the fear of One who can "destroy both soul and body in hell," and instead of fear we feel only magnetic love toward that One, we are free indeed.

CHAPTER 3

"TO SIFT YOU LIKE WHEAT ..."

(Life's a Party, but You're the Piñata)

"For sale. Baby shoes. Never worn."

—What Ernest Hemingway reportedly wrote when a fellow
barfly challenged him to write a great short story in six
words. Hemingway considered it his best work.

Since brass, nor stone, nor earth, nor boundless sea,
But sad mortality o'er-sways their power,
How with this rage shall beauty hold a plea,
Whose action is no stronger than a flower?
O, how shall summer's honey breath hold out
Against the wreckful siege of battering days,
When rocks impregnable are not so stout,
Nor gates of steel so strong, but Time decays?
O fearful meditation! Where, alack,
Shall Time's best jewel from Time's chest lie hid?
Or what strong hand can hold his swift foot back?
Or who his spoil of beauty can forbid?
O, none, unless this miracle have might,
That in black ink my love may still shine bright.

— William Shakespeare, "Sonnet 65."

A month ago our crazy-making gray cat, Penny, survived, barely,
the worst experience of her life. Among her many other peculiarities

(including, but not limited to: scream-meowing in our basement every day for no apparent reason, defecating on the concrete five inches from her litter box for no apparent reason, and sneaking outside to hide out of reach under our deck for no apparent reason) she's absolutely terrible at cleaning herself after she "does her business," as my wife's family likes to describe you-know-what. In short, there's what we'll call "crusty matter" hanging off her haunches on most days.

Finally, Bev couldn't take it anymore and decided (with no regard for what others were doing at that particular random moment, I have to say) to grab that cat Penny and clean off her hinterlands in the bathtub. At first my older daughter, Lucy, was recruited for this suicide mission, but she quickly realized she'd have to maintain a perpetual death grip on a fifteen-pound cat as she was plunged into water for the first time in her life, and Lucy was having none of that. So, against my will and despite firm protests that I was *not* going to get involved in this covert operation, I stepped in to manhandle Penny into the bathtub.

While Bev was at one end furiously scrubbing the "particulates" off of Penny's hindquarters with warm water and liquid soap, I was at the other end, desperately trying to hold on to the scruffy neck of an animal who was sure she was about to die. Her eyes bored into me with disbelief and panic as she frantically tried to claw her way out of the jaws of death. But I tightened my grip and gritted my teeth and held on—no small feat, because I'm positive her girth would remind you of Jabba the Hutt. Thirty seconds into this operation she had the kind of look on her face that you'd have if someone was shoving you feetfirst into a wood chipper. She thrashed and growled and dug her claws into my arm while Bev continued to soap up Penny's nether regions with the sort of trademark thoroughness that, in this case, we honestly couldn't afford.

And finally, when it was all over, we pulled that pathetic, fur-soaked Penny out of the tub and wrapped her in a warm towel and stroked her head and told her that we loved her. I'm no cat whisperer, but I'm pretty sure she was thinking what you and I would be thinking if we were a pampered, half-crazed house cat that had just emerged from her first "acid" bath:

"What was that?"

Now it's weeks later, and Penny still slinks from me whenever it looks as though I might actually make a slight movement in her general direction. Her trust in me has been violated by a shattering event her mind can make no sense of—the comfort and safety she assumed around me has now been cross-examined and thrown out of court. Before her bathing, I was merely just another piece of useful furniture to her. But now I am dangerous and untrustworthy to her. I can see she's having trouble, intense trouble, squaring the food-supplying, head-scratching, lap-offering *me* with the incarcerating, torturing, and suddenly random *Me*. If I was like a god to Penny—albeit a god who's expected to serve her every whim with perpetual consistency—then the bath incident has apparently turned her into an agnostic. A few more episodes like this one, and she'll go the distance to atheism.

So, how do *we* typically make sense of the inexplicable near-death episodes in our own lives? What do we do when God seems to be dipping us in acid or shoving us into the wood chipper, with His supposedly merciful face inches from our own and His eyes locked on ours, and all of our desperate protestations and life-or-death cat-erwauling gets us nowhere with Him? In fact, many of us would say that His grip on the scruff of our necks gets even tighter the louder we protest. Bob Krulish says: "My assumption is that God wants to stand between Satan and me: 'Gosh, I thought you'd fix my marriage. I thought you'd keep Satan out.'"[1] Even when the trauma is behind us and we're safe and enveloped in our metaphorical warm towel, we can't forget or forgive the horrific offense of what He has done to us (or, at the very least, *allowed* to be done to us). We, like Penny, can't square a God who describes Himself as good and lov-ing with the indefensible atrocities of our own stories, let alone the universal abominations of the Holocaust, the Khmer Rouge, the Mexican drug wars, the Indonesian network of human trafficking, and on and on. And don't get us going on the whole natural disas-ter thing—tsunamis, earthquakes, floods, hurricanes, tornadoes, droughts ... you name it. Tom Melton's observation about our apparent paradoxes applies again here—they are only paradoxes to the cat in the bath.

And so, in response to the intolerable dissonance of God's role in our heartbreaks, we decide to live in denial, like the silent wife of a man who's sexually abusing his children. Or we simply ignore aspects of God's behavior that are inexplicable to us, hoping our number doesn't come up on the hardship roulette. Or we try to blot out God from His own story, just as the New Atheists (Hitchens, Harris, Dawkins, and others) have attempted to do. Or we, more and more, turn to the kinds of mythologies that offer sophomoric explanations for the chaotic pain that is part of normal life. Greek mythology, for example, has made a pop-culture comeback, with the Percy Jackson stories so popular that a film version of *The Lightning Thief* was released, barely beating a remake of the campy classic *Clash of the Titans* to theaters. *New York* magazine film critic David Edelstein wrote this about *Clash of the Titans*: "The original *Clash of the Titans* rests on the tragicomic conceit at the heart of many Greek myths: that the seemingly random and often cruel fates of men, women and nations can only be explained by gods and goddesses fighting among themselves like spoiled rich children with too much power."[2] Lacking a sensible explanation for God's reckless behavior, we interpret our random acid-bath/wood-chipper experiences by envisioning our spiritual reality as a locked room ruled by overtired, entitled, hair-trigger brats who treat human beings as collateral damage in their sibling rivalry. Whatever else it is, this is a cowardly and immature response to tragedy.

We must face the truth ... because the truth will set us free.

What the Farmer Knows

When Jesus tells Peter that Satan "has demanded to sift you like wheat," the "you" here is plural—He's speaking to *all* of His disciples. He begins His short discourse with the singular ("Simon, Simon") but then moves to the plural, making what He's about to say a universal truth. Sifting, then, is a *given* in life and an expected reality for all the disciples of Christ throughout history. You can't point to a Christ follower, not a *single one* in the long trajectory of the church, who has not been sifted. And our reactions to the universal sifting we must endure in life are at the core of most of humankind's great music, poetry, prose, art, and filmmaking—they form the essence of our Great Complaint. (To prove the point, as I write I'm listening to

Diana Krall sing the jazz standard "Every Time We Say Good-bye" and the lyric: "Why the gods above me, who must be in the know, think so little of me they allow you to go."[3]) We have all felt the pain of sifting, and we crave explanations and commiserations from our artists and philosophers and even our scientists. We are hampered in this because those of us living in the Western world no longer have an intimate understanding of the agrarian metaphor—*sifting*—that Jesus used with Peter and the others in that upper room in Jerusalem. For them, that word must have carried a kind of thudding weight that escapes those of us who get our food from grocery stores and restaurants and vending machines and therefore know next to nothing about the hard brutalities of the food chain.

When I was in journalism school, working my way through college as a newspaperman and editor, I won a competitive internship at the Colorado state capitol. For a summer I worked in the lieutenant governor's office, creating print and video resources for the state's Rural Council. A few weeks into my internship, my boss decided to leverage my experience as a videographer—he asked me to shoot, edit, and produce a short documentary on rural issues in the state. So I loaded the hulking broadcast-quality video camera equipment into my bright orange 1969 AMC Javelin and set off for a two-week journey around the state, stopping in rural areas to interview and stay with farmers, ranchers, and small-business owners. As a typical suburban-born entitlement baby, I had no clue what life was like for most who carved out a living from the land. The trip was my two-week grad school in the rhythms, hardships, and profound joys of the agrarian life. I learned why farming is one of the most dangerous occupations in the world—there's an intrinsic hardness to almost everything a farmer does. It is hard physically, emotionally, and spiritually. Farmers know that control is an illusion when your outcome is often determined by the capricious whims of the weather. Farmers experience hard things and know they must do hard things on a daily basis. And they are not ignorant about the violence inherent in sifting.

I learned that the basic mechanics of sifting have not changed in three thousand years. It's the violent process of separating the useful from the unnecessary—the crushing and sorting of something whole for the purpose of isolating its nourishing core from the trappings that guard it. In the case of wheat, the kernels are first violently pulled from their stalks—what has so far anchored them in their existence. In Jesus' time the kernels were then repeatedly beaten by hand, but now they are smashed between stones or iron rollers. Mechanized sifting systems beat the kernels, then vacuum them into a venting system before dumping them into a large accordion-like box (the sifter) that violently gyrates. The remnants of the kernel drop through a screen in the bottom of the sifter while the unusable chaff, sticks, stones, dirt, and other pollutants are captured and thrown away. Before mechanized sifters, and typical of the process in Jesus' time, workers threw the beaten wheat husks in the air (a process called "winnowing") or into a sieve to liberate the kernels from their "prison."

The principles of sifting (a beating that's followed by a basic separation that produces a revelation of something valuable) are embedded in our reality—they are all around us, even if we have "no eyes to see" them. For example, I've watched a front-end loader dump a pile of dirt on a loud, gyrating screen that's sloped to the ground. Large clods and rocks roll off, and the filtered dirt falls down under the screen. I've panned for gold by scooping up the sand from a cold streambed and rhythmically swishing water around the pan to separate the lighter elements from the heavier gold nuggets. The sluice box used by nineteenth-century gold-rush miners operates on the same principle. As does the ball mill—a large cylinder with a heavy spinning ball inside that's used in the gold refining process to reveal the heavier gold nuggets hiding in an ore sample. And even the word *tribulation* is rooted in an agrarian reference to sifting—the "tribulum" was a threshing sledge with iron teeth embedded in its underbelly. Its purpose was to remove the husk of the grain by friction and tearing.[4]

Beat. Separate. Reveal.

Applied metaphorically to our lives, as Jesus did with Peter and His disciples in the upper room, the essential effect of sifting is a violent separation followed by a beautiful revelation—sifting shakes us apart for the purpose of destroying our complacent wholeness and revealing what is valuable and permanent and needed. In this case, Jesus reveals that Satan has asked to sift not just Peter, but all of us. Lucifer's motivation, of course, is to destroy us and, by doing so, to separate us from the love of God. He does not understand, and has never understood, that "what [he] meant [for] evil … God [intends] for good."[5] He does not understand the intrinsic truth that "[nothing] will be able to separate us from the love of God, which is in Christ Jesus our Lord."[6] *Turning ugly into beauty* is not a mere commentary on what God does; it is an explanation of His genius and a summation of His redemptive strategies in our lives. George MacDonald writes: "It is the kindest thing God can do for his children, sometimes, to let them fall in the mire. You would not hold by your Father's hand; you struggled to pull it away; he let it go, and there you lay. Now that you stretch forth the hand to him again, he will take you, and clean, not your garments only, but your heart, and soul, and consciousness."[7]

So the men in that upper room, well aware of how a sifting operation actually works, must have felt chills race down their spines when Jesus used the word to describe what was about to happen to them. And Jesus, far from standing in the way of the sifting Accuser, acts like a bullfighter and waves him on. It will be the most devastating assault on his identity Peter has ever experienced. It will produce the same magnitude of despair that later drives Judas to suicide. Even so, Jesus looks him in the eye and matter-of-factly predicts Peter will be there when the dust clears and the sifting is finished. He will, Jesus assures, return to "strengthen his brothers." But Peter misses that prognosis—he flashes at the suggestion that he will shrink from his mission and break his word. Jesus' assessment is, simply, unreal to him. We might as well expect him to agree that the sky is really orange, or that all men are born with goat's feet. Impossible.

So he reasserts: "Lord, with You I am ready to go both to prison and to death!" (Luke 22:33). And Jesus leans in, inches from his face, and cuts him with the truth: "I say to you, Peter, the rooster will not crow today until you have denied three times that you know Me" (v. 34).

Peter has heard Jesus hurl unpardonable epithets at the Pharisees—the kinds of cultural profanities that will get you killed when you direct them at those who have the power to lynch you. He's even heard the words "Get behind Me, Satan" spat at him—but nothing Peter has ever heard Jesus say is more explosive and profane than this retort. No description could be more offensive to a man like Peter than to paint him as a coward, a cut-and-run poser—the kind of Barney Fife nebbish who struts around, talking a big game, but can't get his gun out of its holster because his hand is shaking with fear. The encounter is humiliating, just as it certainly would be for you or me. But on the basis of this truth our lives turn—we enter into the brutality of our sifting and emerge roughed up into the light, into our buried-but-true identity, ready to join Him in His work of redemption.

It's vital to observe that this interchange happens in the context of an ongoing discussion among the disciples about "greatness." It's the longing of our days on earth—*Does my life really matter?* Do I have greatness in me? Or, minimally, have I impacted anyone well enough to inspire passion, loyalty, and respect? Our midlife crises (both the male and female flavors) are always and certainly about a crisis of identity: "Will my life matter in the end, because the end isn't so far away as I've always imagined?" Even more, *every* assault we endure in life is ultimately an assault on our identity—it has always been this way since the time of Adam and Eve, who betrayed God after the Accuser first attacked their Creator's identity and then their own. God is great, and God is good, and we were made in His image—our natural state is to reflect His glory. That's why we hunger for greatness; it's a distant echo of something that was once fundamentally true about us. And that reflection is intimately tied to the fruit that our lives produce. We're hardwired to enjoy making a good impact in the world. The crisis comes when we suspect that we are not. So, it's no surprise that this quiet debate about greatness among the disciples morphs into a loud and divisive argument before Jesus, hours from His agony, must step in. He punctuates the debate by revealing His prerequisite for joining Him on His epic mission....

Sifting.

Beat. Separate. Reveal.

Satan's request, as far as we know, was to do to Peter what he did to Job—destroy everything he held dear in the belief he would curse God when it was all gone. So Satan intends to crush Peter, to target and decimate what he most values: Peter's identity as a loyal-to-death follower of Jesus. In the crusher, Satan expects to expose the *nothing* he's sure is at Peter's core, thereby wounding the heart of God. He believes Peter is all husk, no kernel. It is his fundamental belief about you, too. But Jesus is sure Satan will, instead, find a *something* at Peter's core—a bedrock of love that is not conditioned by his shame. Peter hints at what Satan will discover *after* his sifting when he responds to a plaintive question asked by Jesus and recorded by John. After the crowds abandon Him because He insists that they "eat the flesh of the Son of Man and drink His blood" (John 6:53), Jesus surveys His remaining disciples and asks: "You do not want to go away also, do you?" (v. 67). And Peter plants his flag in the ground: "Lord, to whom shall we go? You have words of eternal life. We have believed and have come to know that You are the Holy One of God" (v. 68–69). My translation of Peter's response is, simply: *"I don't know what 'eat My body and drink My blood' really means, and a lot of what You do and say is a mystery to me, but You've ruined me for You."*

In his submission to National Public Radio's "This I Believe" project, former Sacramento police chief Robert B. Powers writes:

"Once, as a child, I became tortured with the thought that my father might abandon me in a strange city. I told him. He said, 'That's impossible because of love. I couldn't leave you, Rob, if I wanted to. Love is stronger than the trace chains on a twenty-mule team wagon.'"[8] Peter loves Jesus, but Satan's driving belief is that his teams of twenty mules will collapse under the strain of his sifting. It's a simple projection emanating from Satan's own experience as a poser and a betrayer—a being who found only evil at his core when he was sifted himself. He's convinced that all of God's creations are similarly flawed and empty at their core. And he demands the right to prove it.

In the Ring with a Metaphor

The benediction hymn "Panis Angelicus," taken from "Sacris Solemniis" by Thomas Aquinas, describes the blurring of metaphor and raw reality:

> *Bread of Angels,*
> *made the bread of men;*
> *The Bread of heaven*
> *puts an end to all symbols:*
> *A thing wonderful!*
> *The Lord becomes our food:*
> *poor, a servant, and humble.*

When I first heard the words "The Bread of heaven puts an end to all symbols" it reduced me to rubble—that is a perfect description of Jesus' impact on our lives. I mentioned in the chapter "Just a Little Night Music (A Kind of Preamble)" that this book is an experiment in drilling down into the words and phrases Jesus uses, based on the reality that Jesus can convey infinite meaning in His words because He is the master of language. We treat words as if they were spoons; Jesus dispenses them as if they were wells. And there's a similar truth at work in the metaphors Jesus uses. He often teaches using metaphors, expressly because the realities He's trying to convey about the kingdom of God require translation—after all, He's speaking to us of life in a "foreign land."

Artists are quite adept at using metaphors to convey a thing's essence. Film director Steven Soderbergh, in an interview with *Fresh Air* host Terry Gross, explains why he asked actor Matt Damon, in *The Informant*, to deliver his guilty character's courtroom mea culpa as if he were at the Oscars: "Because I knew that part of [the character] liked that kind of attention. And so I wanted to have a sense of the pleasure of that, and it contributes to the fact that [the character] is often disconnected from the context in which he's operating. You're always trying to find the right metaphor, to give somebody an idea [of the truth]. And for some reason I thought of him standing up there sort of with an Oscar in his hand—and what would that sound like?"[9]

Soderbergh's attention to metaphors is legendary. The Oscar-speech "hook" gives Damon the framework he needs to capture his character's peculiar way of thinking. Jesus, however, is not merely good at picking His metaphors—he uses them *perfectly*. He is an Artist "beyond category," the term Duke Ellington used to describe a truly great jazz musician. So whatever metaphor Jesus picks to describe a truth is the *perfect symbol* for that truth—the best container for a kingdom-of-God reality in our human "jar of clay" language.

In fact, His metaphors so transcend symbolism that they *become* the thing they describe, just as Aquinas suggests in "Panis Angelicus." This is a crucial understanding as we drill down into the metaphor of sifting. The mechanics and properties of sifting *perfectly describe* the crushing, separating, and revealing momentum at work in our own stories, because it's the metaphor Jesus chose.

The truth of this hit me again the day I visited former heavyweight boxing champion DaVarryl Williamson at his Denver gym. My friend Charity is a marathon runner, well used to pushing her body to its limits. But last year she was looking for a new and more challenging approach to training, and a friend invited her to try out Williamson's boxing-based training program. She was hooked immediately by the intrinsic *hardness* of the experience, the same way marines who've survived boot camp know something the rest of us don't. Charity introduced me to DaVarryl, who invited me to watch him at work. So I parked my car in a fenced-in lot in a rough-looking part of town I never visit, then walked down a dirty back alley to a steel staircase that led up to an unmarked white door.

Behind that door is Williamson's sweat-soaked gym, with a regulation ring and space for classes to train on the bags. He shook my hand and introduced me to Laura, who was there for a private workout. Williamson—who got his nickname "Touch of Sleep" because he wins most of his fights by knockout, not because he tells boring stories—is a natural-born sifter. An imposing man at six foot two and 220 pounds, with lanky-long arms coiled at his side, his mission is to help men and women "man up," which is another way of saying he beats, separates, and reveals.

Laura—slight and middle-aged with a mop of curly-blond hair—is warming up in the ring by jumping rope, and I make it even harder for her by asking questions about her experience: "Can you describe the impact this training has had on your life?"

"DaVarryl pushes you to be the best you can be," she says between huffs and puffs. "Physically, I've lost fourteen pounds. Emotionally, it's made me much more confident. I was always so shy, so I've always come with others to the gym—today is my first private lesson. That should tell you something. He brings me to a different level."

"How does he do that?" I ask.

"He's motivating because he doesn't lie to you ... *ever*. In today's society everyone gets a blue ribbon—we're supposed to say that everyone is doing good. But when DaVarryl tells you that you did good, you *know* you did. I've tried everything—Pilates, spinning, Jazzercise—but nothing has changed me like this."

As an afterthought, she adds: "One thing for sure is that you will sweat like crazy in here."

As Laura fulfills her own prophecy a few feet away, DaVarryl leans against the ropes and tries to describe the symbiotic relationship between boxing and sifting: "Boxing is different from any other sport or discipline—football, basketball, lacrosse, or a musical instrument," he says. "Those other things, you might need time to find out whether or not you like them. But with boxing, you find out right away whether it's something you want to do. Either I'm going to man up and fight through this, or I'm going to put my head between my legs. So I push people beyond their comfort level. I'm on point—I'm smack-dab on point. I'm as accurate as I can possibly be in terms of their progress. I categorize everyone as individuals. I have a vision of where someone is right now, then what that person can be. I sincerely care about each person who comes in here, but I'm brutally honest because it makes them better."

I ask DaVarryl why some respond so well to his methods while others taste them and never return.

> It's a psychological concept—people genuinely want to do good. When you walked through the alley to get here, you see that it takes a special person to even come in here. I treat people who live in million-dollar houses and people who sleep on someone's sofa the same way. I also treat the women as good as I treat the men. We only do one kind of push-up or one kind of pull-up here. That's the only way we can get the results we need—and I want results. Nathan is a good example—he's lost seventy-two pounds from March to March. He's also started boxing for real—three amateur fights. And it's saved his marriage. Why? Because it gives you a certain swagger. People who were shy and bashful are now more confident. If they can survive this, they can survive anything. It's almost like you're in a foxhole and you've survived a firefight. One wife told me her husband used to be so mean. But this training really changed him—he wasn't mean anymore. He was too tired to be mean. People sit in their car in the parking lot and almost pee in their pants because they're worried about what I'm going

to do to them that day. They have no idea what I'm going to put them through—because I don't tell them what I'm going to do.[10]

By now Laura is plenty warmed up, and DaVarryl is ready to shift gears—he climbs into the ring and straps a pair of boxing gloves on her hands, then pulls on his own pair of trainer mitts. Now I don't exist to him—for the next forty minutes I watch DaVarryl beat down, separate, and reveal Laura. And ringside I'm typing furiously, skipping over DaVarryl's barking demands for punch combinations but capturing most of his high-volume (!) commentary about her performance. Here's a faithful sampling:

> No! No! Get over there! Stay low! Come on, come on! Stay down! It's too high! You're going the wrong way! There you go, girl—give it to me!... Come on! No, your right hand stinks. Beautiful, that-a-girl. Now do it again. I want more speed on that. I want more a** than arm. Better, do it again. Come on, come on! Ugly, ugly, ugly. Beautiful, that-a-girl. Good! No, too high! Move, why would you stay there? Come on, more a** in that right hand. No, the right hand is weak—it's weak! *(Now moving into her space, he forces her to circle and defend herself.)* Too high, start again! I can't accept it! Lower! Right there, even lower. Look at yourself in the mirror—I want it right there. That-a-girl. Whatcha got for me? I want more speed! Good! Whatcha got for me,

baby? That's what I want, I don't want anything less than that. That's too high, Laura, too high! That-a-girl! Punch, Laura! Give it to me! Go straight, not over the top. No, it's unacceptable! Come over here! That-a-girl, that was beautiful. Stop being lazy! Do it again! Come on, I need two-three! *(DaVarryl begins quickly shuffling around the ring's perimeter, while Laura tries to chase him down to attack and jab as he moves.)* Come on! Give me some work! Die for me! I want everything! Come on! Come on! You can cry in the car.[11]

And now DaVarryl is chasing Laura around the ring again: "Move again! Move again!" She's shuffling around the edge of the ring trying to fend off his blows. He stops, and then she chases him around the ring, trying to land two jabs to his chest, like a predator-hamster hunting down a grizzly bear. Now, almost forty minutes into this, she's exhausted and can barely lift her hands to punch. He's relentless. He doesn't even glance my way, but yells to get my attention: "Rick, it ain't my fault! It ain't my fault!" And then: "No, you're trying to get all the power from your back! I want it from your a**! The punches that hurt are the punches you don't see." And just before he yells "Time!" Laura can barely speak and she can't remember what DaVarryl is telling her to do. She's so broken and exhausted she can't think straight. And still he comes at her, taunting her to fight and punch and move ("That-a-girl, do it again!"). When she finally lowers her gloves she is drenched in sweat and her eyes have the far-off look of one who's been dragged through hell.

DaVarryl does one thing very, very well—he delivers a payload of sifting fear into Laura's life in an atmosphere of trust. It's not safe, but it's good—just the way C. S. Lewis described Aslan/Jesus in the Narnia books. It's not safe because she's throwing punches at a heavyweight champion who's not fishing for compliments or appreciation—if he's going to make a fighter out of her, he must give up his need to be liked. And he doesn't stop pushing her when you or I would most certainly stop. He adds layer upon layer of challenge; it all looks like way too much to a bystander like me, but it speaks to the deepest places in Laura's soul—she feels *respected* in a foundational way by DaVarryl. His voice is intimidating and booming and dismissive and then, suddenly, full of passion and admiration. I can see him forcing something in Laura to the surface, a "me" she didn't know was there. He does not treat her with the kid gloves we expect of our gentlemen; he is rough and gruff and, then, surprisingly tender for a moment.

And he is more like God than he knows. At the end, as I'm leaving, I tell him so. And he smiles and stretches out his hand to shake mine and says, "It's truly an honor to have anything I do compared to something in the Bible. Thank you, sir."[12]

The Lurking Melody of Our Sifting

Dallas Willard says, "Tribulation is a word for everyday life."[13] The tracelines of our sifting experiences are in the drip-drip-drip of our common existence and in the epic transitions of our life's arc. We find them in our childhood and in our just-yesterdays. It is not hard to spot them because our soul is tattoo-seared with them.

I will never forget when I was a junior in high school, and the friendship "posse" I'd been with since I was in sixth grade disintegrated.

As we got older, my friends wanted, more and more, to get involved in stuff that made me uncomfortable—vandalizing homes at night, going to see films that were too explicit for me, drinking, and even experimenting with drugs. Finally, after I'd bailed early on a Friday night "adventure" with them, I told them the truth: "Guys, I just don't feel comfortable anymore doing the stuff you like to do. It's just not me. And I can't go out with you anymore. I'm sorry." Far from sparking an honest conversation about our friendship, my best friends—the guys I'd known better than anyone for years, and who knew me better than anyone—turned on me. They spread lies about me at school and even harassed my little sister in the hallways. They spray-painted obscenities on our garage door and publicly mocked a serious illness that I'd had. Years of friendship degenerated into literal hatred overnight.

So, heading into my senior year of high school, I was weighed down by a great sadness, facing an uphill climb to build a new community of friendships from scratch. I felt lonely, rejected, scared, and exhausted—just as Laura did at the end of her forty-minute session with DaVarryl. On a lark I joined the school newspaper staff just so I'd have some place to connect, and there I found a community of friends who were whip-smart, hilarious, irreverent, and full-hearted. They enjoyed and reveled in the artistic *me* that had rarely come out to play when I was with my old friends. And those relationships planted the seeds for my future life as an artist—a teacher, pastor, writer, and editor. The whole experience was heartbreaking and unendurable—even now, there's a sadness in me as I write about it. But it *revealed* me.

Meanwhile, in the just-yesterday category of my sifting experiences, here is what preceded the three-hour drive to the secluded monastery retreat house where I've written most of this book. As I leaned in to kiss my wife good-bye I saw that unmistakable far-off look in her face—a kind of stony distance that told me something was wrong. I asked her, with veiled trepidation, what was going on.

"Nothing ... you need to go."

"No, I'd like to know if there's a problem before I leave for three days."

"There's no time to discuss the problem right now."

"I can take the time—let's go to the bedroom so we can talk in private."

I closed the door and asked her if the problem was with me. "Yes," she cautiously ventured, "but we just don't have the time to talk about it." I said I'd much rather know than not know—it would be hard for me to have it hanging over my head for three days when I'm trying to pour out my heart into this book. Finally, she relented and revealed the problem—our friend Jill had told her as she was leaving our house that I seemed distant from her sometimes, and that I'd acted as if she didn't exist on a couple of occasions. Jill said it humbly, shifting the blame to herself, letting me off the hook. But my wife told her: "I know just what you mean—he sometimes does that to me and the kids, too." An hour before this bedroom conversation I'd tapped Bev on the back at a school assembly to get her attention, and she leaned toward me with irritation and tersely said, "I don't like it when you touch me like that—do it gently, with tenderness." Now I knew why my innocent gesture (at least it seemed innocent to me!) had hit a hot button with her. She'd just heard her best friend talk about how distant I'd been on a couple of occasions, and it reminded Bev of how I'm brusque and far away and disengaged and lacking in tenderness at times—it had poked at the wounds I've left on her heart.

And so, I responded to this helpful feedback just the way you'd expect. I defended myself and flashed irritation at her for expecting perfection in me—for not giving me the space to be human. I was taking on so many difficult challenges on behalf of our family, I argued—breadwinner, father, coach, health-care advocate, tutor, teacher, church leader, lover, writer, payer-of-taxes, cleaner-of-litter-boxes, hauler-of-trash, washer of dishes, and on and on. How, I insisted, was it fair to dump this expectation of perfect engagement at all times on me? And as I built my exacting case for the defense, pleading my innocence to the invisible fairness jury in our bedroom, her face grew hard before she blurted: "You know, what Tom did with me on Friday night was so humble—he asked me if there was something he could do to change the way he approached me so that my encounters with him weren't so intimidating. I wish you could do something like that right now instead of defending yourself." And I sat on the bed and took the bullet, tears welling in my eyes as I finally let what she was trying to say get past my "Not Welcome" mat. She'd skewered and exposed my defensiveness, a protective reflex for my insecurity—*thanks a lot.*

I left home trying to pick my way through the harsh afterglow that *beat* and *separate* always produce—my recommended daily dose of sifting. Three hours later, after the storm in my soul had crashed and bellowed and moved on down the valley, I could see my own horizon again and the beauty of the setting sun—a *revealing.* The fragility of my insecurities was replaced with the tensile steel of God's mercy. I could look myself in the face again.

There is a weight to our ongoing redemption that is unmistakable and leveraged by sifting. We all crave the fruit of redemption in our lives—the "bleeding charity" and the revelation of the hidden treasures of our soul—but few of us invite the kind of heft that's necessary to do the job; it's most often thrust upon us. And the unmistakable sign—the diagnostic observation—that you're caught up in a season of sifting is the sense that hard things are piling up in your life. It's DaVarryl not-asking-but-demanding that Laura keep punching when she had no punch left at all. Most of us can handle one hard thing—we can all take our best cut at a pitcher's fastball, even if we whiff on it. But sifting is more like the experience of a dozen pitchers throwing fastballs across our plate, and us wildly swinging at them just to keep them from hitting us and hurting us and maybe killing us.

People who are experiencing sifting in their lives almost always reference some variation of the phrase I just used—"piling up." We expect to deal with disappointments, frustrations, and even tragedies in our lives. It seems "fair" that we have to face a difficulty or two in the course of grasping for what we've been told is our inalienable right—the pursuit of happiness. But when hardships start to pile up like a poisoned layer cake, well, that's not "fair" (my own case in point is the list of "rock-eating termites" I included in the introduction to this book). And it's this lack of fairness that really—*really*—rankles us. That's exactly why sifting has the power to leverage us so deeply.

For years I've helped lead a national conference for youth workers that is infected, like an epidemic virus, by a tangible Spirit of healing. It's called the Simply Youth Ministry Conference. Our strategy is to offer participants world-class training as a ruse for inviting them into a raw experience of intimacy with Jesus. And so many over the years have told us that they, like the girl Aravis in the Narnia story *The Horse and His Boy*, were chased down, captured, wounded, and then set free by a God intent on removing their husks and revealing their beauty. They wouldn't name it this way, but the cycle of *beat-separate-reveal* and the melody of *ugly-into-beauty* permeates their experiences. Last week, a few days after our conference ended, a woman named Sandy Spittka sent me this email:

> My husband is a full-time youth pastor—we have been in youth ministry for twenty years now. After numerous years attending smaller conferences, we decided to give the Simply Youth Ministry Conference a try last year…. We were not sure really what to expect, but the conference absolutely blew us away! It was incredible—we were so refreshed, and after "one of those years" in ministry, it was just awesome! The Sunday of the conference we met my little brother and his wife for lunch. They lived in the … area, and since we live out of state, we knew we had to see them. We had a wonderful lunch together, laughing and catching up.
>
> We left the conference refreshed, challenged, and ready to tackle ministry once again with a new-found passion. But at lunch that day my brother mentioned he'd not been feeling well and didn't have much of an appetite (a waste at Mongolian

BBQ). Three weeks after the conference—on March 25, 2009—he found out he had two types of aggressive cancer. The cancer was in his liver, bile duct, and had metastasized to his lungs. One week later—on April 1, 2009—my little brother Scott went to be with his Lord and Savior, leaving behind a wife and three small children. He was thirty-two years old.

My world literally spiraled out of control around me. Scott loved the Lord with his whole heart; he served him in children's ministry and as a deacon. He was an awesome husband, father, and brother. I have five siblings, but he was the rock that held us all together. Life literally came to a halt for me. For the rest of the spring, summer, fall, and into winter I was angry. Angry at God, angry at life. We sacrificed so much to serve him, Scott and Laura sacrificed so much to serve him. Scott saw things in black and white, and always stood even when it cost him ministries and friendships. He really was my hero.

Now, I would do the things I had to do as a pastor's wife—attended church, went on summer mission trips, worked with the teens—going through the motions because I knew I had to. I also knew that the problem was with me. God hadn't changed, this hadn't surprised him, but frankly I didn't care. I just wanted to be mad at him. For months I would open

my Bible because I knew that was what I needed to
do, then stare blankly at the pages. I couldn't pray.
There were no words.

God, of course, knew all this and stood by waiting, quietly waiting, for me to find my way back to
him. Right before this year's conference … I knew I
had to do something, so I decided to start a women's
Bible study. That first week felt like standing in a
waterfall after being in the desert for so long. Then
we came to the conference. Again, not knowing
what to expect … and feeling a little like this is where
everything went wrong last year, we came, and every
word spoken by [your team] … was God speaking
directly to me. The circle had been completed. The
worst year of my life … came full circle. I will always
miss my brother. I will always have the questions
of why. But I have again found my passion—once
again know there is nothing I want to do but serve
an awesome God in youth ministry.[14]

Beaten. Separated. Revealed.

One of Tom Melton's "Tom-isms" is: "That which is most personal is most universal." It's both theologically and experientially true.
My stories of sifting, I've found, are both different from and the same
as others' stories of sifting—unique songs, but with the same melody
lurking. I read Sandy's story the same way I listen to a new song on
the radio—but it seems like a song I already knew. I pray for the needs
of people in our church who ask the staff and elders to intercede for

them. As I've already mentioned, every week I get an email that lists these needs—it's essentially an open window into the private, everyday tortures of the people who make up my larger community of relationships. As I write today, the email tells me a woman has asked for prayer because she's sick with a bad virus and is in desperate need of a job. Another has asked for prayer because his mom passed away over the weekend—a terrible blow on top of the discouragement he's been feeling over his yearlong unemployment. And another has asked for prayer as he prepares to testify in court against his former boss. Behind each of these one-sentence requests hides an epic story of sifting that is personal to them and universal to me.

It would be hard to have a real conversation with pretty much anyone in your life and not run across a story of sifting that seems vaguely familiar to your own story yet distinctly *other*. The first sentence in *Anna Karenina,* Leo Tolstoy's great, tragic novel that chronicles the consequences of both sin and faithfulness, is: "All happy families are all alike; each unhappy family is unhappy in its own way." Likewise, every story of sifting chronicles a unique unhappiness but produces an "alike" bounty. And the melody embedded in each of our distinct songs of sifting is ugly-into-beauty, ugly-into-beauty, ugly-into-beauty.... Steve Hartman, the CBS News feature reporter with a deft touch for human-interest stories, is best known for his ongoing series "Everybody Has a Story." Every other week Hartman would throw a dart at a map of America, travel to wherever the dart hit, and then profile someone picked randomly from the phone book. His basic premise was that there is an epic story—a story worth telling on national TV—embedded in every person's life. I couldn't agree more. And, drilling even deeper, every epic story (and every hero, as F. Scott Fitzgerald observed) is leveraged by an experience of sifting.

William Paul Young is just one example of this truth. He's a hero to many after the book he originally wrote only for the benefit of his children, *The Shack*, became one of the best-selling works of fiction ever, selling more than twelve million copies in its first two years. I'd already read and admired aspects of *The Shack* when I saw the unedited video footage from an hour-long LifeTree Café[15] interview with Young. Young's story, I quickly learned, was no typical path to success—it had all the familiar rhythm of *beat, separate, reveal*—a monumental sifting that formed the foundation for a heartbreaking and ultimately redemptive story.

The Shack, as many already know, tells the story of the abduction and brutal murder of a little girl, and her father's subsequent confrontational encounters with all three members of the Trinity in the desolate mountain shack where the girl was imprisoned and killed. Young's aim was to embed in the story his own howling questions about the apparent contradictions between the "good" in God's goodness and the hammering brutalities he'd experienced in his own life. In his protagonist, Mackenzie, the grieving and furious father, Young channels the melting of his own frozen soul—the by-product of a childhood dominated by abuse and disconnection.

In the interview, Young describes his heartbreaking roots as a missionary kid in Papua New Guinea, with a father who was a severe disciplinarian and "addicted to the work of God." Before he was six he was effectively being raised by adults in the primitive tribe his parents were trying to reach, listening to them debate whether they were going to kill his mom and dad and experiencing sexual abuse as a normal part of life. At six his parents sent him to a boarding school where the older boys continued to molest him. After four months at the school Young returned home for a short visit, calling his mother the generic "Aunt Betty" (a name used for any white woman) even though her name was Bernice. In his short life his most important connections, and even his fundamental sense of safety, had been shattered.

Young grew up and entered the ministry, where he perpetuated the survival skills he'd learned early on: Perform to maintain an appearance of connection, lie about what's really going on in your soul, and keep your addictions secret. But those skills could not stop the relentless parade of heartbreaks. During one six-month period Young's fifty-nine-year-old mother-in-law died suddenly and his eighteen-year-old brother and five-year-old daughter were both killed. Later, his wife discovered he'd been in a three-month affair with her best friend, and his marriage was now on the chopping block. These "great sadnesses," as Young calls them, are funneled undiluted into *The Shack*. And that, he says, is one big reason the book has found such a large audience: "I think the book resonates with a lot of people who have great sadnesses. It can be the loss of a child, it can be the loss of a spouse, ... it can be medical issues, or the loss of a dream. There [are] many things that we can have great sadness about ... [when] we just don't understand what happened."[16]

Here, of course, he's exactly describing the *beat-separate-reveal* experience of his (and our) long confinements on the threshing floor. It is a high-stakes gambit, shocking in its brutality, no doubt, but transformed into an adagio by the "maestro of hope," to use my friend and Youth For Christ Vice President Dave Rahn's description of God. Young describes the ugly-into-beauty melody that runs through his story's refrain:

> [At one point] I lost all my hope because [my wife] Kim had hammered on me until I was standing at the edge of the cliff looking down into this big hole of all my junk. She's yelling at me, "Deal with it, let's just deal with this!" I'm looking down in there and I'm thinking: *What am I supposed to do? How do I go back to before I was four years old and find something that's real? What about my life is not a survival mechanism or a safety skill?* I didn't think there was anything [about me] that was real. And I'm thinking, *I've puked on every relationship I've ever had—my kids would be better off without me.* And I'm planning a trip to Mexico so that I can kill myself without my kids being able to find my body.
>
> And God miraculously shows up in the form of two friends. One went up to Kim and said, "If you keep [metaphorically] hitting him you are going to kill him." The other one came to me and asked, "Where are you?" And I explained all [that I'd been thinking], and I said, "I'm just a piece of crap—I'm just dried up and blowing away and I'm terrified there won't be anything left." And this woman who is our friend said to me, "Paul, there's a seed." A seed. But I'm thinking, *A seed?* A seed. Okay. I'm

thinking, *You know, if there's a seed, if there's even just a seed of something, then it could grow. I don't know what it is, but it could grow.* Then I think, *You know, seeds, they grow good in this kind of stuff.*

And suddenly all my hope came back. The last time in my life I was suicidal was that day. And I've been suicidal my whole life. It's the grace of God. Every bit of this is the grace of God.... Kim was furious for the first two years [after the revelation of my affair]. And it took eleven years for us to heal. I went into counseling and began to work on this stuff and I knew for the first time in my life that I couldn't heal myself. And I knew religion couldn't heal me either....

At the end of eleven years, I'm one of the healthiest people. I have no secrets. There's nothing my family doesn't know. I have no skeletons in my closet. I have no reputation [to protect]—that came out with the secrets, you know. I am the same person in every situation. I'm no different sitting here than with my friends or speaking or in a hotel room by myself. I am the same person. [A year and a half ago, Kim and I were] sitting in front of a group of friends—and they all [knew] my history.... And she says to them in front of me, "I never thought that I would say this in my life, but it was all worth it."[17]

Beaten. Separated. Revealed.

These words—"it was all worth it"—are shocking to Young and to us. Considering our own stories of sifting, we want nothing to do with "worth it" platitudes unless they're uttered, in Young's case, by a wife who has opened her heart wide again. Rather, we determine, nothing could *possibly* be worth all of this. And here we embrace-without-understanding one of the great mysteries of our lives with God, and of Peter's experience of Jesus—what our heart affirms ("it was all worth it"), our head refuses to acknowledge ("nothing is worth this"). If the wheat kernel had a soul, the beating of its sifting would not feel like a good thing, of course. It would feel like piling on—a death in a bathtub. In fact, the whole thing would feel unendurable and inexplicable. But if the wheat kernel had a heart it would sense, on the back end of its sifting, that something simultaneously new and ancient is just barely visible through the settling dust and chaff. It would discover, as if in a moment but really in a thousand moments strung together, that "beauty will rise."

Sifting Reveals, It Does Not Create

In an interview with talk-show host and media empress Oprah Winfrey, U2's mercurial lead singer, Bono, describes the mystery of a beauty that is revealed, not constructed:

> Oprah: Can you set out to write a hit and then actually write one?

> Bono: Well, one of the things that hits have and that great music always has, you know—the music feels like it was already there.

Oprah: Like your song "Beautiful Day."

Bono: I don't know if that's great. But when you stumble on certain melodies, you think, *that was already there.*

Oprah: It's like what Michelangelo said: The sculpture was already in the stone.

Bono: And I don't think he was just being clever. The hit—what might be called eternal music, if you want to be high-minded—is a song that most people feel familiar with. And the most extreme end of that spectrum is music...

Oprah: ... that resonates on a level that's indescribable.

Bono: Right. Like "I've got sunshine on a cloudy day." Or my favorite song, "Amazing Grace."[18]

The *you* that is revealed through your sifting experiences is the "eternal music" of your true identity. But the revelation of our *already there* beauty is no simple process—we are, like King David in the Old Testament, a toxic mash-up of "great music" and the noises a nine-year-old makes when she's learning clarinet. How to turn the volume up on one and mute the other? My favorite Christian band is The Normals, a three-album, flash-in-the-pan collection of musicians that, for me, still represents the high-water mark for music that is insidiously redemptive. The lyrics to their brilliant song "Black Dress" describe the subtle beginnings of the cycle of sifting at work in the soul of David, the tarnished golden boy:

> *I'm drowning in desire*
> *I've been good for so long*
> *I know I've got no right now*
> *But no one can tell me that I'm wrong*
> *Will she wear that black dress?*
> *Will she wear that black dress?*
> *As holy as the night*
> *As holy as I want to feel*
> *I want to feel all right*
> *Maybe I'll be good*
> *I could be gone when she gets here*
> *I've still got a chance to make this one all right*
> *My temptation's on the stairway*
> *My temptation's at the door*
> *My temptation is before me*
> *She is standing before me in that black dress*[19]

And here begins the shocking descent of the Old Testament's most compelling and influential heroic figure. Over the years I've heard many struggle to join the two apparently dichotomous "arcs" in David's life—the valiant, tender, and wise "man after God's own heart" and the conniving, murdering sexual predator whose children and wife despise him. It's as if our dissonance forces us to treat him as two different people—good David and bad David.

Author and former priest Brennan Manning says:

> When I get honest, I admit I am a bundle of paradoxes. I believe and I doubt, I hope and get discouraged, I love and I hate, I feel bad about feeling good, I feel guilty about not feeling guilty. I am trusting and suspicious. I am honest and I still play games. Aristotle said I am a rational animal; I say I am an angel with an incredible capacity for beer.
>
> To live by grace means to acknowledge my whole life story, the light side and the dark. In admitting my shadow side I learn who I am and what God's grace means. As Thomas Merton put it, "A saint is not someone who is good but one who experiences the goodness of God."[20]

The "light" and the "shadow" that describe David merge into something whole when we consider his story through the lens of sifting. After he flees Jerusalem to escape death at the hands of Absalom, his own son, David's entourage straggles into the backwater town of Bahurim, where a relative of his old nemesis Saul, an elderly man named Shimei, still lives. In a scene that must have seemed pathetic to the few men of war still loyal to David (including Abishai), Shimei shuffles out of his house in a fury, hurling curses at David and taunting him ("worthless fellow!") while tossing little stones at him. Abishai, appalled at David's total acquiescence to this treatment, has had enough: "Why should this dead dog curse my lord the king? Let me go over now and cut off his head" (2 Sam. 16:9). But David's response reveals the separating power of the sifting that has already beaten him to a pulp: "What have I to do with you, O sons of Zeruiah? If he curses, and if the LORD has told him, 'Curse David,' then who shall say, 'Why have you done so?'... Let him alone and let him curse, for the LORD has told him" (v. 10–11).

The more we are reduced and reversed into helpless children in the midst of our sifting, the more likely we are to see God as capricious; because we are children, we lack the perspective to see Him any other way. But for those who hang by a thread to the goodness of God—those who have "tasted and seen that the Lord is good"—the sifting has the volatile leverage to mature our souls, making it possible for us to see God as He is, not how we wish Him to be. David follows his rebuke to Abishai with this: "Perhaps the LORD will look on my affliction and return good to me instead of his cursing this day" (v. 12). David has started the turn toward the revelation of his soul—to the moment before his death when he famously declares:

> The LORD is my rock and my fortress and my deliverer;
> My God, my rock, in whom I take refuge,
> My shield and the horn of my salvation, my stronghold
>   and my refuge;
> My savior, you save me from violence.
> I call upon the LORD, who is worthy to be praised....
> He sent from on high, He took me;
> He drew me out of many waters....
> He also brought me forth into a broad place;

He rescued me, because He delighted in me. (2 Sam.
22:2–4, 17, 20)

Beat-separate-reveal.

The man who dragged himself through every degradation
known to man—who sacrificed his identity like Esau giving away
his birthright for "a mess of potage"—emerges from the beating and
the separating of his sifting to proclaim a stunning revelation: "He
delight[s] in me." Only a man revealed can say such a thing. And
only a man revealed can see God for who He is. Jesus describes the
mystery of sifting's power to reveal God when He tells the thousands
gathered on a hillside for His first sermon, "Blessed are [the purified]
in heart, for they shall see God." On one side of our sifting, to use
the apostle Paul's metaphor, "we see in a mirror dimly"; on the other
side, we see "face to face." Before, we "know in part"; after, we "will
know fully just as I also have been fully known" (1 Cor. 13:12). The
knowing fully goes hand in hand with the *being fully known.* It is a
revelation of God and of ourselves—a revealing that, finally, settles
something in our souls.

In his novel *David Elginbrod* George MacDonald writes:

> Many things were spoken by the simple wisdom
> of David, which would have enlightened Hugh
> far more than they did, had he been sufficiently
> advanced to receive them. But their very simplic-
> ity was often far beyond the grasp of his thoughts;
> for the higher we rise, the simpler we become; and
> David was one of those of whom is the kingdom of

Heaven. There is a childhood into which we have
to grow, just as there is a childhood which we must
leave behind; a childlikeness which is the highest
gain of humanity, and a childishness from which
but a few of those who are counted the wisest
among men, have freed themselves in their imagined progress towards the reality of things.[21]

We can't see God as He is when we are trapped in "the childhood
which we must leave behind." Again, King David's experience of sifting fuels his understanding of this reality when he writes, in Psalm
92:6–8, "The senseless man does not know, fools do not understand,
that though the wicked spring up like grass and all evildoers flourish,
they will be forever destroyed. But you, O LORD, are exalted forever"
(NIV). Yes, evil is all around me, but God is good.

Sifting helps us say good-bye to the inexplicable and unpredict-
able god of the nursery and say hello to the ferocious, tender, playful,
and shrewd Lover that He really is—one glimpse of Him this way,
and we are ruined for every other lesser god. Like the princess who is
rescued from the tower by a dragon-slaying prince, we can't help but
give ourselves—body, mind, and spirit—to our rescuer. "I once was
lost, but now I'm found," exulted John Newton in the song he wrote
to celebrate his sifting—"Amazing Grace." We no longer own our
own heart; it is His to ravish because He's the one who has found and
revealed it…. And now, when He calls us by name, we feel a tingle
down to our toes. Author Dan Allender sums it up well: "You have
been damaged. But you have great hope. The mercy of God does not
eradicate the damage, at least not in this life, but it soothes the soul

and draws it forward to a hope that purifies and sets free. Allow the pain of the past and the travail of the change process to create fresh new life in you and to serve as a bridge over which another victim may walk from death to life."[22]

In the story of Job and in the story of Peter, Satan is given permission to sift but not to grind—the next step in the processing of the wheat kernel into flour. Grinding must happen before you consume, and Jesus does not allow Satan to *consume* Job or Peter or you or me. The essential "work" of sifting is revelation—it reveals; it does not create. And what it reveals, again, will seem like a new thing about you but feel like an old thing about you. The seventeenth-century mathematician and theologian Jacob Bernoulli, widely acknowledged as the father of probability theory, had these Latin words inscribed on his headstone: *Eadem mutata resurgo.* Translated, it means: "Though changed I shall rise the same." Yes, sifting seems to change us, but only because it reveals us. And that revelation will bring the kind of fundamental change that will, to play with Allender's image, deconstruct your old "bridge to nowhere" and help you to start functioning as a "bridge to somewhere."

Historically and biblically and personally the *beat-separate-reveal* cycle is a deeply *positive* process, even though no "spoonful of sugar" will help this medicine go down—it pretty much tastes like death. But the *reveal* in this cycle is a moment of beauty that extends into a lifetime of beauty because that's what happened in Peter's story, and in my own story, and in the stories of so many others. That doesn't mean, however, that the reveal we experience always appears as a warming sunrise—the moment just before the sun's light begins to break over the horizon is, of course, also the darkest of the night. That is true simply because God has embedded the created world with metaphors that are intended to remind us of how things work in His kingdom (Rom. 1:18–20). So when my wife exposes my defensive insecurities, I'm not tempted to break into a Mexican hat dance. That moment is dark. And for so many of us, our seasons of sifting are darker than dark. That's why the reveal is such a shock when it comes.

Revelation brings a blinding light where there has been darkness. And when the light comes on in a dark and long-neglected place, you're likely to feel physical pain as your eyes try to adjust. You're also likely to find a lot of ugly you didn't even know was lying around in your soul. Because He so "respects His creation," as William Paul Young affirms, God chooses to clean house in a well-lit room where we—not just Him—can see the dirt. And He shoves a broom into our hands and says, "Let's get busy." So the revelation at the back end of your sifting may not seem, initially, at all positive or good or "worth it all." I'm fairly certain that the eleven years it took to bring healing in William Paul Young's relationship with his wife was often a wincing plunge into the light. I'm also certain that anyone who can say "it was worth it all" after a season of sifting is naming one of the true joys of life—the revelation of who we really are and who God really is.

Somehow the sifted, separated, and revealed have tasted God's colossal goodness in a way that is unique to them and universal to all. I can never say on behalf of another that her sifting was "worth it all"—that's offensive. But I can say it for myself, and the "another" can say it for herself. God's goodness is not a comparative goodness— He's not good to me in relation to another's more dire circumstances. When He is working His goodness into us as a baker works leaven into dough, it's as if He has blinders on. He's not distracted by all the other globs of dough sitting there in his bakery, waiting to be kneaded. His omnipotence and omniscience make it possible for Him to work His goodness into my life as if I'm the only "glob of dough" He has His hands on. The good I experience in Him is deeply personal, even though I can taste the same leaven in others' "dough."

The point of all of this is that many, many of us who have known what it's like to be sifted will not be doing the Mexican hat dance anytime soon either. But if you are in the cycle of sifting right now, or have been, the revelation of your untarnished beauty promises to set you free and make you exclaim, as the apostle Paul does, "I consider that our present sufferings are not worth comparing with the glory that will be revealed in us" (Rom. 8:18 NIV).

CHAPTER 4

"BUT I HAVE PRAYED FOR YOU, SIMON ..."

(The Fundamental For-ness of God)

He had ever one anchor of the soul, and he found
that it held—the faith of Jesus. (I say the faith
of Jesus, not his own faith in Jesus.)
—George MacDonald, *Robert Falconer*

God is a comedian playing to an audience too afraid to laugh.
—Voltaire

But is a mustard-seed word—a tiny container of plutonium that, effectively deployed, can produce the kind of impact that leaves behind a mushroom cloud. In linguistic terms, *but* is a "coordinating conjunction"—when Jesus uses it here with Peter it functions as a spotlight that, formally, "indicates a contrast or exception."[1] *Does it ever.* But, of course, we've seen some pretty nuclear *buts* indicating "contrasts and exceptions" thrown around in history....

Marilyn Monroe famously proclaimed, "I'm selfish, impatient, and a little insecure. I make mistakes, I am out of control, and at times hard to handle. *But* if you can't handle me at my worst, then you sure as hell don't deserve me at my best." On the eve of war, the Spartan king Leonidas implored his troops, "Give them nothing! *But* take from them everything!" The poet Maya Angelou, reflecting back on her life, said, "I've learned that people will forget what you said, people will forget what you did, *but* people will never forget how you made them feel." Jimi Hendrix, acting the sage, advised, "Knowledge speaks, *but* wisdom listens." Theodore Roosevelt reminded us, "Criticism is necessary and useful; it is often indispensable; *but* it can never take the place of action, or be even a poor substitute for it." John F. Kennedy grabbed that baton: "As we express our gratitude, we must never forget that the highest appreciation is not to utter words, *but* to live by them." And, of course, Anonymous warned, "The early bird gets the worm, *but* the second mouse gets the cheese."

These "contrasts and exceptions" deliver a payload of declaration— *but* is the Saturn V rocket of the English language. And the rocket Jesus launches when He uses *but* with Peter threatens to destroy His best friend's fundamental trust in His kindness. Peter's expectation, just like ours, is that Jesus is his advocate, not his enemy. If Satan demands, Jesus will rebuke. If the Liar insinuates, the Truth will expose him. If the Thief creeps in to steal, the Shepherd will drive him away. So this *but* is an earthquake, akin to advising an innocent man on death row, "Your lawyers have pursued every avenue of appeal, *but* …" Jesus is contrasting everything He's said before with everything He's about to say. And there is no bigger demarcation in history.

Embracing the Dark Side

A couple of years ago we were camping with some friends at a mountain park about an hour from our home in Denver. There's nothing like the bracing peace of a crisp mountain morning, with the sun filtering through the trees and the smell of bacon cooking over a stove. I had a cup of steaming coffee in my hand. The birds were yammering at each other. The air hitting my lungs was seasoned with pine. My wife and daughters were still asleep in the camper. And the couple who owned the camper were sitting twenty feet away, observing their morning ritual—they'd been marching through the Bible together every morning before their workday took them in separate directions. Their "Two-Year Bible" broke the Scriptures into day-sized chunks. This particular morning they were reading aloud Joshua 10 and 11, Luke 16 and 17, and Psalm 63.

I thought a little Scripture reading would be the perfect soundtrack to my isn't-God-great morning. So I recalibrated and turned my attention away from the sounds of chirping birds to the thud-thud-thud of the Old Testament. What I heard was disturbing, to say the least. Joshua 10 and 11 is a brutal, maybe even violating, account of God's plan to wipe out the armies and kings that dared to threaten His people. As Joshua and his army prepare to engage the armies of the five Amorite kings who'd defied God and marched on Joshua's allies in the city of Gibeon, God tells His servant, "Don't give them a second thought. I've put them under your thumb—not one of them will stand up to you" (Josh. 10:8 MSG). Later in the chapter, after Joshua has decimated the enemy armies and driven their kings into the bowels of a cave—where they cower, awaiting their doom—he orders his men to drag the kings before him, then "put [their] feet on the necks of these kings" (v. 24 MSG) as a kind of object lesson. Joshua then proclaims to the gathered victors: "Don't hold back. Don't be timid. Be strong! Be confident! This is what GOD will do to all your enemies when you fight them" (v. 25 MSG). And then Joshua executes the kings and hangs their bodies in five trees where they stay all day and into the evening, when he orders them pulled down from the trees and thrown back into the cave where they'd hidden before, sealing it with large rocks.

Honestly, standing there next to the camper, trying to reclaim my punctured peace, I fantasized about those birds having a volume control, because I would've cranked it.

But I couldn't escape the carnage. All the way through the end of chapter 11 it's story after story after story of the same thing. The sound of this suburban middle-aged couple calmly reciting two chapters of graphic bloodbath, directed and enabled by God, sucked all the romance out of that bright mountain morning. It was an exercise in macabre repetition. *But no worries*, I told myself, *I'll just endure until they finish with all that Old Testament brutality and start up on the "give peace a chance" New Testament.* But as soon as they'd launched in to Luke 16 and 17 I got a snootful of the same—here, Jesus tells the story of the rich man and Lazarus. The point of the story is that there's no mercy for a coldhearted and arrogant fat cat who's missed the deadline for his repentance. The man dies before his blind eyes finally see the error of his ways, so he's doomed to a gnashing agony … for eternity. This is not on the approved list of stories for children's church. But it merges perfectly well with Joshua 10 and 11. Turns out, when you're simply reading the Bible in random chunks it can be positively disconcerting.

My morning was saved from the precipice because, thank God, the couple's reading of Psalm 63 was nothing like the ground they'd already covered. Here I heard King David's thirst for God—his unabashed praise of Him:

> O God, you are my God,
>   earnestly I seek you;
> my soul thirsts for you,
>   my body longs for you,
> in a dry and weary land
>   where there is no water.
>
> I have seen you in the sanctuary
>   and beheld your power and your glory.
> Because your love is better than life,
>   my lips will glorify you.
> I will praise you as long as I live,
>   and in your name I will lift up my hands.
> My soul will be satisfied as with the richest of foods;
>   with singing lips my mouth will praise you.
>
> On my bed I remember you;
>   I think of you through the watches of the night.
> Because you are my help,
>   I sing in the shadow of your wings.
> My soul clings to you;
>   your right hand upholds me. (vv. 1–8 NIV)

Now, I'm thinking, *I finally have the kind of Scripture passage I was craving this morning—something grateful and good and happy.*

And that certainty lasted for all of thirty seconds, right up until my friends capped off their reading of Psalm 63 with David's matter-of-fact postscript:

> They who seek my life will be destroyed;
> they will go down to the depths of the earth.
> They will be given over to the sword
> and become food for jackals.
>
> But the king will rejoice in God;
> all who swear by God's name will praise him,
> while the mouths of liars will be silenced. (vv. 9–11 NIV)

Okay, then …

Old Testament, New Testament, Psalms—all randomly chosen but eerily tied together by a jagged thread. And all of them read aloud in the *we're-reading-the-Bible-now* fashion that is familiar to Christians everywhere. I mean, we're often in lockstep through cataclysmic passages in the Bible, reading Scripture the same way we read Shakespeare in junior high—with a kind of labored distance. We would never read the police reports of a gangland slaying this way. We'd be appalled by the carnage and the casual viciousness.

But we don't really give ourselves the option to act appalled by God's movement and will. Because God directed it, the carnage morphs into cartoon violence—like the campy old TV show *Batman*, one of my favorites when I was a kid: "Biff!" "Pow!" "Ouch!" God has a dark past. Jesus has a dark side. Yet David can't get enough of Yahweh, and I'm drawn to Jesus like no other. Intimacy with Him is not only the "endgame" for the Christian life; it's the greatest, grandest thing we can experience. He's not only good, He defines good. So how do we square His dark side with that? We're confused and scared by God's brutality—we're compelled to overlook or ignore or deny His dark side, but we just can't do that. If we deny what is plainly there in Scripture we confirm that something about God needs to be covered up—to be overlooked and even camouflaged. And there is nothing about God that should not be known. He's not embarrassed or ashamed about anything He's done or is doing right now ("'For my thoughts are not your thoughts, neither are your ways my ways,' declares the LORD" [Isa. 55:8 NIV]).

I was well into my marriage when, in a casual conversation with my parents over the phone, my mom revealed to me a random act of purging: They had, she told me, suddenly been afraid that their kids would discover certain letters between the two of them that they had saved in a box in their crawl space. What would happen, they reasoned, if they were both to die suddenly, leaving me and my two sisters to go through their things as we prepared to sell their house? Well, we might find these letters and read them. And then we would know things about them that would change, apparently forever, the way we saw them. So, in uncharacteristically dramatic fashion (for those of English stock), my parents took those letters and threw them into their wood-burning stove. Of course, I would never have known they did this had my mom not called to tell me what they'd done. She revealed this purging because they were trying to protect us from something they were sure would harm us—that's what parents do, right? But I told my mom that, actually, I would've preferred to know what was in those letters because it would've helped me to understand them better. I told her I wasn't afraid of experiencing the truth about who they are. I was disappointed and sad about their preemptory strike against the dark truths of their life. And not knowing those truths left me more, not less, distant from them.

No, we can't run from God's dark side. To "know Him fully," *we must run toward it.*

And, as I've said, if we can't look at His behavior with a bare face, with matter-of-fact honesty, then we are fundamentally affirming that there is something scary and abusive about Him that must be covered up. If the adult children of an abusive father insist on describing him as an incredible man, free of faults, they are affirming him as a monster. They reveal their unspoken fears when they repress what is plainly true about him—when they frame him as the man he is not. It's a self-serving, though understandable, deceit; hidden monsters are likely to kill you if you expose them. And it's impossible for little children to embrace their parent as an abuser, because that would make life intolerably dangerous for them. The same dynamic is at work when we turn a blind eye to what is plainly true about God's behavior in the Scriptures—we decide we can't afford to see Him as a psychopath.

But if we can assess God's behavior honestly—examine Him in the light, not relegate Him to the shadows—then we disable the fear that keeps us functionally distant from Him. In 1 John 4:18, the disciple "who Jesus loved" says: "There is no fear in love; but perfect love casts out fear, because fear involves punishment, and the one who fears is not perfected in love." When we run toward God's dark side, we lay down the fears that have kept us from true intimacy with Him.

Embracing the Brutal

Jesus' *but* is brutal. And it's jolting, at first, to see "brutal" used in any descriptive way with God. I know this. But I've used "brutal" *not* for its shock value. There is an aspect of God's behavior—as described in the Bible and experienced in our lives—that we can translate only as "brutal." Like many other words we use to describe our experience of God, it's not really true, but it's accurate. Here's what I mean: When I tell my seven-year-old daughter she can't have a friend over because it's almost dinnertime, and she calls me "mean," her description of what I've done is not true, but it's an accurate way of describing her experience of me. I'm "mean" because I've not given her what she wants, and she can see no good alternate reason (including "dinner's ready!") to explain my decision. When a girl I briefly dated after college told me, bluntly, that I was "too much" for her, she was accurately describing her experience of me, but "too much" isn't a true description of who I am. And when the Pharisees angrily labeled Jesus a "blasphemer" for claiming He was no garden-variety prophet, but the very Son of God, they were not telling the truth, but their experience of His words was "accurate" within their frame of reference. In the same way, it's accurate for us to label how God sometimes behaves as "brutal," but it's not true.

Five years or so ago I was slowly realizing that I'd compartmentalized God for most of my life—I did not (could not?) understand the stories about Him, or His dealings with me, in an integrated way.

No one had been more tender or kind to me in my life—there's a greatness to God's love for me that is palpable and … *fundamental*. There are tears I need to cry that release only when I'm alone in His presence. There are raw places in my heart that only He knows how to access and nurture. There are secrets about my soul that only He can speak to. But He has a fearsome and nearly inexplicable side—revealed in Joshua 10 and 11 and everywhere else in the Bible—that I didn't know what to do with. It's as if I was offered a five-course meal of God and told the waiter to take the beet-and-brussels-sprout salad back to the kitchen; I'd rejected the parts of God that made me feel sick to my stomach. And here's something that served only to deepen my dissonance: I'd experienced a deeper love than I've ever known from Him during times of great brutality in my life.

Finally, the dark tension that immersed my soul because of these apparently dichotomous experiences of God was resolved, at least a little, when I turned my focus away from Him directly and onto the world He created. In Romans 1:18–20 Paul explains: "The wrath of God is being revealed from heaven against all the godlessness and wickedness of men who suppress the truth by their wickedness, since what may be known about God is plain to them, because God has made it plain to them. For since the creation of the world God's invisible qualities—his eternal power and divine nature—have been clearly seen, being understood from what has been made, so that men are without excuse" (NIV). Paul is revealing a reality that my own curiosity and experience undergird: The whole world is a parable (a metaphoric treatise) describing God's character and personality. His "invisible qualities" and "eternal power" and "divine nature" are clearly seen and understood by "what has been made." Paul is saying that all created things are inherently a living biography of God—they tell God's story, the makeup of His character and His kingdom, for those who will pay attention.

So I began to study the created world, specifically considering the microdetails of living things. Soon I realized the created world is full of contradictions and extremes that remind me of God's apparently dichotomous character:

- God created butterflies—soft and fluttery and beautiful and harmless ... and He also created hornets.
- God created dolphins—cute and friendly and helpful and brave ... and He also created sharks.
- God created rainbows—comforting and colorful and beautiful and awesome ... and He also created the weather patterns that produce hurricanes.
- God created puppies—soft and eager and happy and lick-y ... and He also created grizzly bears.
- God created Jimmy Fallon ... and He also created David Letterman.

I realized I was pretty sure what butterflies and rainbows and puppies and dolphins were telling me about the God who created everything, but what were the hornets and hurricanes and grizzly bears and sharks trying to tell me? Isaiah heard God remind him: "Your ways are not My ways."[2] That's not the platitude we've turned it into—it's a permeating truth as deep as the universe is wide. His love is *heavy*—broader and more fearsome and *other* than we have imagined or allowed ourselves to embrace. And we experience this heavy love as if—as the apostle Paul says—we're looking into a "dim mirror"; it seems brutal to us, even though "brutal" is not the truth about Him. But there is a weight to brutality that is matched and reflected by the weight permeating God's love. And, it turns out, the specifications required for our redemption are far heavier than we usually acknowledge. God's grace, the heaviest weight in the universe, has been rendered featherlight by our persistent sense of entitlement. We often treat grace as if we could pin it on our lapel like a button, when it's actually as hard and as imposing as a boulder: "He who falls on this stone will be broken to pieces, but he on whom it falls will be crushed" (Matt. 21:44 NIV).

We can't understand the need for the weight of grace unless we understand the context for its necessity. So a short history of our redemptive reality is crucial.

At the beginning of all things the ever-existent Trinity and the created angels are lounging on heaven's equivalent of the back deck, enjoying one another. But a rebellion is brewing, and it leads to a war in heaven. Lucifer, the leader of the rebellion, is defeated and thrown down to earth, where he prowls for his prey, like a wounded and desperate carnivore. He manages to deceive God's treasured son and daughter, fouling their pristine hearts with lies and egotistical pipe dreams. The Enemy pollutes and twists their hearts, mortally wounding their relationship with God—by rights, Adam and Eve belong now to "the kingdom of darkness." And so God loses His beloved, who now hide from His presence, breaking His heart ("Where are you?" [Gen. 3:9]). But God hatches a plan to win them back. The campaign will have to be shrewd and *forceful* (in Matthew

11:12 Jesus says, "From the days of John the Baptist until now, the kingdom of heaven has been forcefully advancing, and forceful men lay hold of it" [NIV]). Force and heft will be necessary because what has happened has cracked the universe—rent it in two by the most brutal of blows.

We have never really understood the *mass* of the break caused by Adam and Eve's first sin. This gash in the universe will require *heavy love* to heal. So God first institutes a brutal system of animal sacrifices for the atonement of His beloved children's sin and betrayal. Living, breathing animals are executed, and their blood is poured out on the altar as a repeated substitute for the penalty of our betrayal. This system builds a bridge for relationship, but is only temporary (though the Enemy, of course, doesn't know this). It's a mere precursor—or more accurately, a *sleight of hand*—necessary for the deft maneuver that will follow. The Enemy needs to understand this system of brutal exchange as God's "endgame"—as a flawed system that he will, in time, leverage and overcome. And so, with the Enemy so distracted, God unleashes His masterstroke; He sends His own Son, like a paratrooper landing behind enemy lines, as willing bait for a final sacrifice, which will effect a cataclysmic reversal of the breech. And the Enemy, the Destroyer, senses the surface truth that this Jesus is a threat, so he targets Him for destruction. Lucifer shows up in the desert to tempt a weakened Jesus using a trusted strategy—he will appeal to the same primal lust for power and control that bulldozed Adam and Eve into an unthinkable betrayal. But Jesus is having none of that. The Enemy is banished from His presence, where he stays until he sniffs an opportunity to launch a second assault in a lonely garden.

In Mel Gibson's brilliant portrayal of this tipping-point con-
frontation in *The Passion of the Christ*, the weight of the assault is
palpable. Jesus is alone and tormented to the point of death on the
eve of His crucifixion. The serpent moves through the Gethsemane
garden toward the exposed feet of Jesus—now perilously within
striking range. Everything hangs in the moment. And then, in a
shocking burst of violence, Jesus stomps on the serpent's head.[3] It
is sudden and brutal and … revelatory. It turns out that Jesus—
sweating blood, abandoned, and apparently beaten—is no shrinking
violet. The Great Surprise is that He cannot be leveraged and that He
is no victim of circumstances. In this, He is not at all the way most
Americans describe Him.

I once decided to find out what young people fundamentally
believe about Jesus, so I had camera crews all over the country stop
teenagers on the street and ask them to describe Him. When I got
the raw footage from these interviews back, I quickly noticed that
these young people—no matter their socioeconomic or ethnic
background—*all* used one particular word to describe Jesus. And
that word is *nice*. This experiential insight is backed up by the most
in-depth research ever done on Americans' religious beliefs and
behavior, which discovered that most of us relate to God as if He's
our benign "cosmic servant"—an obedient, forgiving, backslapping,
attentive "divine butler."[4] But is this the Jesus who can bring the heft
that's needed into this dark battle?

Perhaps my favorite adventure in life (outside of my marriage)
has been guiding ministry leaders on an eight-hour exploration into
what Spurgeon calls "making a beeline to Christ." I've called it "Jesus-
Centered Ministry"—it's an approach to ministry that treats Jesus

not like the "cup-holder accessory" He's become in the church, but
as the engine who drives everything. When I get to the point in our
journey where we must grapple with Jesus' "nice" reputation, I show
them a short video clip from the start of *Mister Rogers' Neighborhood*,
the legendary TV show for children that featured the cardigan-clad
Fred Rogers greeting viewers by singing "It's a Beautiful Day in the
Neighborhood." Then I tell them that, to most children and adults in
our culture, Jesus looks a lot like this man. He's unfailingly nice. And
then I use a metaphor to describe how most people in our culture
experience life at one time or another—as if they're alone in a bad
part of town, lost and wandering down a dark alley where thugs
sharpen their knives in the shadows. And, given that fearful reality,
I ask them who they'd prefer to be walking by their side down that
alley. "Not Mister Rogers, that's for sure," is the common answer.
And then a realization settles over the room like a hard frost—we
have led people to believe that Jesus is a fundamentally nice person
who, like Mister Rogers, would get torn apart if He walked with
us into our scary dark alleys. Of course we have trouble trusting
Jesus with our lives—it's a firmly rational response if we believe He
is merely "nice." If our collective definition of Jesus is true, then
He can't possibly be the man for this job—the job of our redemption. That will require the kind of serpent-stomping brutality never
practiced by Mister Rogers but quite like C. S. Lewis's metaphoric
picture of Jesus as an untamed lion.[5] If Jesus lacks the weight of
brutality, we are without hope.

Of course Jesus is unbelievably tender and merciful and
kind. He heals and sets free and defends and weeps and humbles
Himself, over and over. But our kind images of Him don't explain

that serpent-crushing scene from *The Passion of the Christ*, nor do they explain the other ways His brutality surfaces: when He drives the moneychangers out of the temple in Matthew 21, or when He tells a Canaanite woman who's begging Him to cast a demon out of her daughter that she's a dog in Matthew 15, or when He calls Peter "Satan" in Matthew 16, or when He tells the rich young ruler in Matthew 19 that all his efforts to master the law are essentially worthless, or when He—time after time—lambastes the Pharisees with words so strong they were considered grounds for execution.

No, the Scriptures tell us that Jesus has come to "destroy the devil's work" (1 John 3:8 NIV) so that He can reclaim His bride, His beloved: you and me. To do it, our very nature must be reclaimed and the great rift in the universe must be healed. Our betrayal must be paid for through the sacrifice of a Lamb with downcast eyes and an air of resignation as He lies exposed on the altar—and who then leaps off that blood-soaked table like Aslan in *The Lion, the Witch, and the Wardrobe* and drives our Enemy into a final exile. Our redemption is accomplished by the brutality of the Lamb—it's an oxymoron that is undeniably true and remarkably reenvisioned in Lewis's Narnia books. I love the scene from *The Voyage of the Dawn Treader* when the bratty, self-centered boy Eustace suddenly finds himself magically turned into a terrible, ugly dragon after he discovers an abandoned pile of dragon treasure and falls into a greedy sleep.

At first the petty and insecure boy enjoys the fear he can now produce in people as he swoops at them, breathing fire. But soon he's lonely, afraid, and miserable as a dragon. And his arm is really hurting because he slipped a dragon-treasure bracelet onto his wrist before he fell asleep, and now it's constricting his much-larger dragon limb.

In the midst of his misery, a large, fearsome lion—Aslan—comes to him in the night. Eustace is afraid of the lion, but not because it threatens to eat him. It's a different kind of fear—the sort you feel when you're in the presence of a Presence much bigger and greater and *other* than you. The lion leads Eustace to a well in the mountains and tells him he must "undress" before he slips into the well's soothing waters. Eustace doesn't understand what it means to "undress" at first because he's, well, already a naked dragon. But soon he figures out that he should try to tear away at his dragon skin to see if he can find the boy still living underneath it. He does this three times, to no effect. Then the lion says: "You will have to let me undress you." Because Eustace is desperate, he lies on his dragon back and exposes his soft underbelly to the lion's claws: "The first tear he made was so deep that I thought it had gone right into my heart," he says. And after the lion tears away the deepest remnants of Eustace's dragon skin, he invites him into the water. When Eustace emerges he's a boy again (actually, a boy redeemed), soon to be dressed in "new clothes" by the lion, who is Jesus Christ in full.[6]

If we have truly met the Jesus depicted in Lewis's story, our response to a question about His fundamental nature would be radically different from "nice." He's no "divine butler"—He's more like the "divine tornado." And that's the "good" in the good news of the gospel. He has, like a highly trained professional athlete, the capacity for brutal strength, but the real mark of that strength is His ability to temper it according to the situation. The strength of His restraint is, truly, the essence of His beauty. The cross isn't beautiful—any more than an electric chair or a noose is beautiful—*but the incarnate God who has submitted His strength to the cross is beautiful.* The cross has been assimilated into our culture as a decoration. This is, really, unthinkable, because the cross is no metaphor—it's the actual means used by ancient Romans to dispense of a criminal in the most unwatchable way humans can imagine. The brutality of the cross hints at the brutality of the battle—the weighty permanence of the very real separation brought on by the betrayal of Adam and Eve. We need a Jesus who will not shy away from the job at hand; the brutal job at hand. Eustace is a perfect stand-in for the ways we attempt to retain a semblance of control in our lives—we'll explore every option to first save ourselves, realizing in the end that we're not able to cut as deeply as we need to, so we give ourselves over to a Lion brutal enough for the job. The beautiful tipping point in *The Voyage of the Dawn Treader* is when Eustace, like us, rolls over to expose his tender underbelly to Aslan, an untamed lion who knows how to use his claws. The *but* of Jesus means He will dig deeper than we ever would. He will use fearsome means we would never try. He will bear all things, believe all things, hope all things, endure all things on our behalf.[7] And His brutal love will "never fail" us.[8]

Pulling the Trigger

In Psalm 23 David comforts a beleaguered and fearful people with this: "Though we walk through the valley of the shadow of death, His rod and staff comfort us."[9] What exactly is supposed to comfort us? Well, the staff he's referencing is a well-known symbol within the shepherding culture so familiar to David—it's a prod for rescuing stray sheep lost or caught up in the brambles. But what about the rod? Again, as all who first read David's words would know, it's the fearsome weapon of a shepherd, made for defending sheep threatened by a predator. That *is* comforting—to think that our Great Defender has a weapon that will fend off our enemies. But what happens when, as is often true, we become our own worst enemy? Will He use His weapon to beat back the enemy within? Will He "comfort us" with the brutality of the rod?

On a Saturday morning a few years ago, my wife was sick in bed and my two little girls were anxiously pleading for me to get my act together so we wouldn't be late for a family birthday party. They were already strapped into the car waiting in the garage. And I was angry. Angry that everything was on my shoulders ... again. My wife has a chronic disease called sarcoidosis that, in the past, rendered her so exhausted she often could not get out of bed. During this particularly bad stretch, before she began an experimental treatment that has restored her strength, I was living at a frantic pace, trying to keep up with my job while handling most of our household responsibilities. I was angry that my wife was sick—but she couldn't help that, I told myself. I was angry at my kids for wanting to be at their birthday party on time—but they couldn't help that, I told myself. So ultimately I was angry at myself, for having an empty tank when I was trying to merge onto my Saturday-morning superhighway.

In my angry, impatient rush I hurried through the door into our garage but missed a last step on the stairs. I did one of those ninety-degree ankle-buckling falls with a hot latte in one hand and my laptop slung over my other shoulder. It hurt. It really, really, really hurt. It hurt so bad that I unleashed the loudest bellow of my life. I pounded the concrete garage floor and let the dam that was holding back all my pain, frustration, and anger burst. Inside the car, my kids watched all of it wide-eyed, like raccoons caught in the headlights.

The garage functioned like an amplifier, making my screams sound even louder. That's when the neighbors showed up—the new neighbors I hadn't even met yet. They'd heard my screams and rushed over to see me pounding the floor in a pool of latte.

"What happened?" they cried.

Right about then my disheveled wife rushed into the garage in her robe and asked the same question. Then she looked up and saw our new neighbors standing there. "Hi, I'm Bev," she said, pulling her robe a little tighter around her. Through my clenched teeth I spit out an inaudible indictment—"What a perfect way for the new neighbors to meet us."

Well, it turns out our neighbors were parents of teenagers and thus well practiced at entering into a crisis. They quickly discovered our girls were supposed to be at a birthday party and offered to take them to the party so they wouldn't miss it. My wife gave them directions while I dragged myself into the house and hobbled to a chair so I could elevate my grapefruit ankle. My wife, who'd stayed away from me that morning because of my aforementioned grouchy behavior, got some ice for my ankle, cautiously gave me a tender-ish squeeze, and left me alone.

In the silence I ran back through all of the things that had gone wrong that morning, like a prosecutor laying out the charges before the defendant. In the dock that morning was God. And in the middle of my complaint God opened His mouth and spoke:

"Rick, I pull the trigger."

He didn't have to say it twice—I knew exactly what He meant. He was trying to say that He's not afraid to use His rod when circumstances require it—that His love is fierce and passionate and unafraid to stop me in my tracks before I do any further damage. He will bring the brutal when it's needed. Of course, I'm not saying He stuck out His foot and tripped me on those garage stairs, and I'm not saying God will beat us up if we won't listen to Him. But I am saying what my soul knows is true: that God is the prototypical "tough love" parent who will not hesitate to put me in "adult time-out." In the silence that morning, with my ankle swollen and throbbing, the tears came. And through the tears I heard Him speak again: "I want you to come away with Me, Rick." He was wooing me again—stopping the trajectory of my macrotantrum so He could offer me, all over again, His fundamental love.

It's crucial to point out here that *everything* God does is subject to love—to the brokenhearted He's a balm, but to the hypocritical or conniving or abusive He's a nightmare. Both responses are acts of love fueled by His redemptive intentions: "Behold then the kindness and severity of God; to those who fell, severity, but to you, God's kindness, if you continue in His kindness; otherwise you also will be cut off" (Rom. 11:22). In all things He wants sons and daughters who reflect Him. And this is why the apostle Mark records Jesus offering this brutal directive: "If your hand or your foot gets in God's way, chop it off and throw it away. You're better off maimed or lame and alive than the proud owner of two hands and two feet, godless in a furnace of eternal fire. And if your eye distracts you from God, pull it out and throw it away. You're better off one-eyed and alive than exercising your twenty-twenty vision from inside the fire of hell" (Mark 9:43–48 MSG).

This disgusting and extreme advice is, obviously, hard for us to know how to live out in our everyday life. But it's not so hard to understand when we see it in light of our Lover's intent. He's telling us to submit to the brutal sacrifice of the *lesser* so that we can gain the inestimable treasure of the *greater*. The greater, in this case, is *Jesus Himself*. He wants to replace our puny love of possessions and esteem and sex and ease and self-actualization and fame with a Great Love—one Love to rule all other loves (to use a Tolkien-ian metaphor). He wants intimacy with us because He's passionate about us and for us. And like anyone who loves deeply, it rends His heart when we prefer our many other base lovers over His own great love. He is, by His own account, a "jealous" Lover—that means He wants us for His own. That's good news for Peter, who hears he's about to be sifted and unprotected from its terrible impact, and it's good news for us, who have seen what the rock-eating termites can do.

We relax in the presence of the untamed Lion—we can walk through the valley of the shadow of death because we have this brutal Lord Jesus walking so close to us that His Spirit inhabits us. He *must* be dangerous … for our own good. Somewhere in our souls we crave the love of a God who's willing to do anything—anything—to reclaim our hearts for His own. Most of us have never experienced this kind of epic passion brought to bear on us—but we do in Christ. God wants His sons and daughters back, and He'll risk all, including our misunderstanding of His words and His character and His intentions and His actions, to rescue us.

Playing with the Tension

There is a palpable tension (or tautness) in the micron between Jesus' *but* and His revelation that "I have prayed for you." He is going to let a hard, sifting thing happen to Peter, but He will be fervently "for" him in the midst of it. Tom Melton frames these apparently dichotomous realities as a "dialectical epistemology"—a formal way of asserting that we learn the deepest truths by embracing what appear to be mutually exclusive thoughts or behaviors.

As I was spelunking in the depths of my own tension over Jesus' "but I have prayed for you," Tom launched me into a long exploration of the great standard-bearer for dialectical epistemology: twentieth-century philosopher, theologian, academic, environmentalist, and author Jacques Ellul, who was a fighter in the French Resistance and later served as deputy mayor of Bordeaux. Ellul embraced the Hebrew sensibility that faith is a tension between extremes—like a person balancing on a tightrope wire, you have no chance of walking on the wire unless it's pulled taut. Likewise, there must be tension in our faith, or we won't be able to live it. There's a perfect example of this dialectic tension in the film *Fiddler on the Roof*, when Tevye sits alone debating his either-ors over the offer of marriage the village tailor has extended to his daughter: "He's beginning to talk like a man. On the other hand, what kind of a match would that be with a poor tailor? On the other hand, he is an honest, hard worker. But on the other hand, he has absolutely nothing. On the other hand, things could never get worse for him, only better."[10]

Ellul defines this dialectic as "a procedure that does not exclude contraries, but includes them."[11] In this, he frames reality as a narrative—a ripping good story—rather than as a linear progression. Only in story can two extremes coexist, because stories are about people, not equations, and the most interesting people we know are full of contradictions that somehow entwine at a miraculous vortex and bowl us over.

My wife is a marvel of surgical clarity in the midst of an intense conflict, but conflict truly frightens her. She will punctuate her full-hearted reaction to the playful tweaks of a friend with a hard slap to the shoulder, and then worry on the ride home that she might have offended her offender. She can be casually critical of people at almost the same moment she's expressing her awe of them. She rarely "gets" my jokes, but when she does, no one laughs louder or longer. She's a natural actress, but she frets over a role as if she's headed for the guillotine. And she's very aware that we live under the constraints of a one-income budget, but the other day she bought $150 worth of exotic sunscreen from the dermatologist (I'm pretty sure I'll get a flying elbow in the shoulder for that one).

My wife is the most beautiful woman I've ever known—and that is true because of, not despite, her many contradictions.

Likewise, Jacques Ellul was captured and intoxicated by two seemingly oppositional extremes in his life—the socialist theories of Karl Marx and the gospel of Jesus Christ, which superseded but did not negate the way Marx saw the world. Ellul embraced much of Marx's fundamental observation that the whole world lives in some aspect of tension (specifically, class tension). These tensions, observed Marx, are unavoidable—they're like labor pains that can advance only through revolution. But it's this last declaration by Marx (advancement comes through revolution) that Ellul rejects in favor of the "advancement" of the gospel. We live in a tension that makes sense only in light of Jesus' death and resurrection. The resolution of the oppositional mysteries we experience in life is, simply, the revelation of Jesus Christ and His perfect mirroring of His Father's heart. Ellul says, "It's only when we understand the Lordship of Jesus

Christ that we are truly free."[12] And a dialectic understanding of the Bible, he explains, acknowledges that "we constantly see two contradictory, apparently irreconcilable things affirmed, and we are told that they always meet to wind up in a new situation."[13]

So, Peter is locked in the dialectical tension between the brutality of Jesus' *but* and the wonder of His intimate advocacy for him—"I have prayed for you." How can these two realities merge? We face the same problem when we consider that God "made Him who knew no sin to *be* sin on our behalf." And, then, we have these everyday dichotomies to sort out:

- Living in the world, but not being of it.
- Loving the sinner, but hating the sin.
- Recognizing that the love of money is the root of all evil, but that money is also a clear token of God's blessing.
- Treating governments as installations of God, but affirming they are not to be obeyed in contradiction to God's will.
- Living under judgment, but counting on mercy.
- Involving ourselves in the political world, but not treating politics as the source of our hope.
- Enjoying an old episode of *Flipper*, but cringing through a repeated viewing of *Jaws*.

That last one was gratuitous, I know….

I've already said that the created world, full of its own dichotomies and tensions, started me on my way to embracing the dialectical tautness of God's behavior. *The Truman Show* completed the journey for me. In this revelatory film, a man raised from birth on the enormous bubble-roofed set of a reality show—where he is the unwitting star of a fully scripted life routed through hidden cameras to a huge TV audience—begins to suspect that nothing in his so-called life is real. All those who populate his acquaintance are secretly actors, paid to make his life "work" while slipping in surreptitious product endorsements. So he has friends who apparently revere him, a wife who apparently worships him, a job that apparently brings out his best, and a life that is apparently free of doubt and sorrow. And slowly he recognizes how tormenting this "perfect life" has become to him. He starts to sense the truth: that his carefree and riskless existence is a sham. And he plots his escape, knowing that he's risking everything—the safety and painless existence that so many of us insist we want—for a chance to have his heart broken and his dreams smashed. In the end, he fools the hidden cameras that surround his life and steals a boat, pushing out into an "ocean" that abruptly ends at the painted wall of the dome. There, he finds a barely noticeable staircase that leads to an exit door. With one last look at the life we have all longed for when our rock-eating termites threaten to collapse everything we hold dear, he opens the door into the dialectical reality, where God is good but God is not tame ... or nice.[14]

When I first saw *The Truman Show*, it occurred to me that the film offers the perfect answer to our central doubt about God's goodness. Truman has what we all want—a "god" who shields us from every threat and who surrounds us with ease. A God who says no to the Enemy when he asks permission to sift us. But, as a result of all this "plenty," Truman's life is emptied of the one thing that makes it worth living—the deep sense that we are freely loved and can freely love in return. In 2 Corinthians 1:8–9 Paul says: "We were really crushed and overwhelmed, and feared we would never live through it. We felt we were doomed to die and saw how powerless we were to help ourselves; but that was good, for then we put everything into the hands of God" (TLB). What a stunner—"but that was good"! And why is it good? Because, of course, under the tension of our sifting "we put everything into the hands of God." We reclaim the trust that Adam and Eve decimated. Under the direst of circumstances, and in the face of our own heartbreaks, we walk the tightrope of trust and faith, offering God the only thing of value we possess: our freedom.

And so the great kindness of God—the brutality of His *but* and the for-ness of His "I have prayed for you"—leads us to repentance (Rom. 2:4). God is unfailingly kind but only sporadically nice. That's true because the nature of His kindness is radically different from its popular and shallow translations. Kindness isn't measured by the act but by its effect. It's hard to diagnose an action as "kind" except in retrospect, when you examine what it has produced in you. My wife once asked me to move out of our house and live separated from her for three months. In the moment, there was nothing kind about this; but as I sit here today, I recognize it's one of the kindest things anyone has ever done for me. In his worship song "Marvelous Light," musician Charlie Hall writes: "I once was fatherless, a stranger with no hope. Your kindness wakened me.... Your love it beckoned deeply, a call to come and die."[15] Is the "call to come and die" a kind thing? For those who've answered the call, and submitted to the sifting, and traded the lesser for the Greater, it is....

Jesus, Peter learns, has had a conversation with the Trinity on his behalf—maybe he was the focus of prayer for Moses, Elijah, and Jesus on the Mount of Transfiguration. Maybe. But why does Jesus tell Peter about His conversation? His prayers need no public declaration to be true. But He reveals to Peter that He has advocated for him to the Trinity because He wants him to hang on to a fundamental and irrevocable truth: that He is an unflinching advocate. In John 17 Jesus delivers what we now call "the High Priestly Prayer"—it's a rambling treatise on His advocacy for His followers, cloaked within an intimate and intercessory conversation with His Father. The strategic purpose for speaking His prayer out loud, among His disciples, is buried in verse 24: "Father, I desire that they also, whom You have given Me, be with Me where I am, so that they may see My glory which You have given Me, for You loved Me before the foundation of the world." Jesus wants us to be with Him. Just as Satan accuses the brethren night and day, so Jesus "always lives to make intercession" for us (Heb. 7:25).

My friend Steve Merritt, a counselor whose practice focuses on teenagers, told me the story of a friend of his who works as a psychiatric nurse at an inpatient mental hospital. One day on the children's unit they were watching a film. One young boy kept asking Steve's friend, "Does the prince rescue the princess?" After the boy had anxiously tugged on her shirt many times, she was moved to kindness and decided to reveal the plot's mystery: "Yes, he gets the girl." Because this boy had been traumatized and broken, he needed to know how the story was going to work out. The tension in his life and soul needed the resolution of hope, just as our dialectical tension can find release only in "the maestro of hope." Yes, we are broken and traumatized by the *but* of God, but the Prince will win the heart of His bride. *"I will find you, no matter how long it takes, no matter how far. I will find you."*

A last little postscript: It turns out that hurricanes literally keep our planet alive by roiling the waters of our oceans so deeply that their nutrients are widely redistributed, causing rapid growth of the carbon-dioxide-eating phytoplankton and, thus, keeping the earth from boiling over.

Everything in the created world is a parable.

CHAPTER 5

"THAT YOUR FAITH MAY NOT FAIL ..."

(The Magician's Mistake)

Take it that a vision would make us sure, it follows either
that God does not care about the kind of sureness it would
give us, or that he does not care for our being made sure in
that way. God will have us sure of a thing through knowing
its source, the heart whence it comes; that is the only worthy
assurance. To know, he will have us go in at the grand
entrance of obedient faith. If anyone thinks he has found
a back stair, he will find it land him at a doorless wall.
—George MacDonald, *Castle Warlock*

Faith never knows where it is being led but it
loves and knows the One who is leading.
—Oswald Chambers, *My Utmost for His Highest*

Sometimes shadows are the only light we see.
—Leo Kottke, "Twice"

On the popular *Mythbusters* TV show, special-effects gurus Adam
Savage and Jamie Hyneman are on a mission to blow gaping holes
in urban legends, conventional wisdoms, and outright fairy tales.
The show's tagline is: "I reject your reality and substitute my

own!" In one gospel-esque segment, Savage sends away for a contraption that looks like an insect and operates like an oversized bicycle—the makers promise that this Rube Goldberg monstrosity will enable the user to "walk on water." So I watch as Savage mounts the thing in a swimming pool, furiously pedaling as he, like Peter so many centuries before him, slowly sinks to the bottom.[1] Peter's attempt to walk on water fails when the faith that drives him overboard into the choppy sea quickly morphs into crippling self-consciousness. Savage's attempt to walk on water is doomed from the start because of misplaced faith—belief is not a commodity that can be "applied" universally, no matter what the marketing claims. (Actually, failure might've been his goal all along—it's much more entertaining.)

Jesus tells Peter that he's going to be sifted. And He tells him He's already prayed for him. And He reveals that His intercession is focused on Peter's faith—that it won't fail him when he needs it most *(forget about that whole water-walking episode)*. From this, we can extrapolate a few things right away:

- Faith is the "vehicle" that will propel us through our sifting, like an armored tank picking its way across a battlefield.
- It is possible for our faith to either succeed or fail.
- Jesus is highly invested in the strength of our faith.

Not long ago I was struggling with a difficult issue related to my career—I was locked in the cramped space of another Ellul-ian

tension. God had asked me to be patient, to wait on the revelation of
His intentions within my dialectical journey, to keep walking toward
Him on the taut tightrope of my faith. But you know how that sort
of enterprise often turns out—I had spotty success. So one day, when
Bev's nurse was in our home to administer her regular infusion treatment for sarcoid, I overheard them talking about my struggles and
their impact on me. Kathy is more than Bev's nurse—because she
spends so much time in our home, and because she's a remarkably
wise and enjoyable woman, she's become our good friend. I heard
Kathy ask Bev: "Well, he's a man of faith, right? Why doesn't he
just exercise his faith that this will all turn out the way he's hoping it will?" She then mentioned that she'd given the same advice to
her son-in-law, a pastor who was struggling over where and how he
should be ministering.

When I overheard Kathy's reaction to my struggles—that I'd
been wrestling with doubt and impatience instead of infusing (!) my
soul with trust—I had a visceral reaction. I said: "Actually, I *don't*
have faith in what God will do for me; but I *do* have deep faith in
who He is." One kind of faith is convinced that, somehow, we've
done everything we need to do so that God can come through for us.
The other kind of faith is more like Job's passionate response to his
friends' assertions that God is out to get him: "Though He slay me,
I will hope in Him" (Job 13:15). The distinction is enormous and
is vital to understand when we consider what Jesus is trying to tell
Peter as he's about to be swept onto the threshing floor. I call Kathy's
implied understanding of faith—that God will do what we're hoping
for if we believe hard enough and sincerely enough that He'll do
it—"Great Pumpkin" faith.

The Fallacy of "Great Pumpkin" Faith

In the classic Charles Schulz Halloween cartoon *It's the Great Pumpkin, Charlie Brown,* Linus, the geeky, overearnest best friend of Charlie Brown, is determined to skip trick-or-treating to wait—all night if he has to—for the mythical Great Pumpkin to show up in his "most sincere" pumpkin patch, where he will disperse gifts to the faithful. Linus convinces Charlie Brown's little sister, Sally, to forego the candy-fest and wait with him. When it's finally apparent that there will be no visit from the Great Pumpkin, Sally blasts Linus in front of his friends, who've come with their overflowing goody sacks to check on them. As they abandon Linus to wait alone in the pumpkin patch, he makes a fatal error—"If the Great Pumpkin shows up you'll be sorry!" he barks. And he is immediately racked with fear and guilt—"Did I say 'if'? I meant when—*when* the Great Pumpkin shows up!"[2] But it's too late for Linus. He knows he will get what he's hoping for only if he betrays no disbelief. He's convinced he must say the right things and do the right things to clear the way for the Great Pumpkin's gift-giving presence—remarkably similar to the way many of us would describe the way faith is supposed to "work" in our lives.

To illustrate the difference between this subtle bastardization of faith and the faith Jesus is targeting when He speaks to Peter, I invited Hunter Helmick, my eighteen-year-old friend who's a professional illusionist, to give a short performance during a sermon at my church. After he'd made a tissue dance in midair, then morphed it into a rose, I asked him a purposefully uncomfortable question: "I bet you get a lot of people asking you how you do these illusions—what if I asked you to tell us how you did that one?" Of course, Hunter said he would never reveal the "trick" behind his illusions—that would ruin the mystery. I've already mentioned that he bristles when people refer to him as a magician—he's an expert at sleight of hand, not a conjurer who's tapped into a well of spiritual power.

Great Pumpkin faith, at its core, uses formulas and insider guidelines to leverage (or trick?) God into doing what we want Him to do. Like Hunter, practitioners of Great Pumpkin faith are working hard to get the "trick" right. It's like the old TV show *Bewitched*, where Samantha the suburban witch wiggles her nose to get what she wants. When we "practice our faith" by concentrating on saying and doing just the right things so we can get God to perform for us, it's a lot like wiggling our noses (and it smacks of the "divine butler" most Americans believe God to be). Faith, in this framework, is a thing to do, not the fruit of our intimacy with Jesus. Trouble is, we much prefer *doing* to *abiding*—we don't even know, we must admit, *how to abide*. But, boy, do we know how to do and do and do.

And this understanding of an *abiding* faith is crucial because it's the key that unlocks a little-explored story recorded in Acts 8—the rise and fall of Simon the magician. Simon has already won renown in Samaria for his Copperfield-like ability to pull off grand illusions that confound the swelling crowds who flock to see him. He earns the nickname "The Great Power of God." His trickery makes him famous and rich. But then the apostle Philip comes to town, leading a band of ragamuffin disciples, preaching "the kingdom of God and the name of Jesus Christ," (v. 12) and baptizing many. And he promptly steals the show from Simon. The magician is so bowled over by the miracles and the message that he, also, commits his life to Christ and is baptized. There is no record of Philip casting out a demon from Simon prior to his conversion, or any reference at all to Simon's being under the power of the Devil. He's an expert illusionist, that's all.

Meanwhile, the disciples in Jerusalem hear about what's happening in Samaria and realize the new believers haven't yet been filled with the Holy Spirit, so Peter and John go down there to lay their hands on them so the converts can receive the Spirit of Christ. Simon, still the huckstering illusionist, is fascinated by this "trick" and offers to pay Peter and John a large sum to gain their secret. Peter, ever fierce, responds by lambasting Simon, telling him that his "heart is not right" and accusing him of bitterness and bondage to sin (vv. 21–23). Peter punctuates his fury with this: "You can't buy the gift of God with money."[3] In fact, we can't *barter* for the gift, either—faith is not a *thing* we can acquire; it's a *knowing* that we act on. I mean, faith is the fruit of a growing intimacy with Jesus that leads to a truer understanding of who He is and what He's intending to do in our lives. Faith, in this sense, looks much like the confidence a long-married couple has in each other. Because they have intimate knowledge of their hearts, they exercise a relaxed faith in each other's character and, therefore, their behavior.

Bev and I have a close friend who left her husband three months ago under extremely difficult circumstances. With her seven-year-old daughter, she first found refuge with friends who had an "apartment" for guests in their basement and a built-in playmate for her little girl. After three months there our friend knew it was time to let her host family get back to their normal rhythms, so she set a deadline for moving out, and we started praying that God would provide a new place for her (with our small home as her "emergency" backup). As she "chewed the cud" on this pressing need, Bev kept thinking of a particular woman in our church who'd been in a Bible study with her five years ago. Soon, because the woman's name continued to surface, Bev started wondering if God wanted her to call the woman—a real step out of her comfort zone after five years of little contact. But Bev thought she remembered that this woman and her husband spend four months on the Jersey shore every year, closing down their large residence in a beautiful neighborhood ten minutes from our home. So, despite her hardwired reservations, Bev responded to the nudge and called the woman; she explained the situation and asked her if she'd be open to a house sitter. The woman was at first taken completely off guard and doubted whether her husband would be open to the arrangement. It didn't look good. Two days later the woman called back and told Bev she'd talked to her husband and wanted to meet our friend. Today we spent the afternoon with them. In a few days we're moving our friend into their place, which is one of the most beautiful homes we've ever seen.

I think this is a perfect example of what Great Pumpkin faith *is not:* Real faith is not about *working up* enough belief to move a lazy or stingy God off His duff. It is, instead, a persistent confidence in the heart and character of God that is sealed by action. What was God's heart toward our close friend? Well, we knew His heart was to provide for her, though we had no idea how He was going to do it. So Bev is persistent in her conversation with Him, keeping her heart open and available to God because she loves and trusts Him. And God, for His part, is also persistent—gently poking at her throughout the day, hoping she will be awake to His nudges. And if she doesn't respond, or misses the meaning of His nudges? He is not harsh—of course, He understands that faith is not a formula but a Person we follow; that it's an art, not a science. He will find another way. Meanwhile, the seed is planted in the hearts of the couple with the beautiful home—they, for their part, honestly pay attention to God's nudges, then respond faithfully by taking a few steps forward. It's the same highly aware movement that happens when we're trying to find the right path in a forest at dusk. We pay close attention, recognize when we've missed the fork in the path, backtrack if we need to, and oodge our way forward.

As messy as all of this is, it strikes me that it's like great jazz—improvisational, surprising, and made possible because of the trust among the "players." Jazz musicians don't play with sheet music in front of them, and faith has no formula.

The Physics of Faith

When Jesus chides His disciples for their lack of faith, it's usually because they *do not understand Him*. For example, after the disciples board a boat with Jesus, intent on crossing the Sea of Galilee, they're suddenly caught up in the vortex of a killer storm (Mark 4). While Jesus is napping below decks, his friends—some of them seasoned fishermen—are panicking. The waves are crashing over the sides of the boat, filling it with water. So they jolt Jesus awake with an indignant accusation: "Teacher, do You not care that we are perishing?" (v. 38). After rubbing His eyes, then stilling the storm with a word, Jesus fires back: "Why are you afraid? Do you still have no faith?" (v. 40). Their response to Him exposes the DNA of their faithlessness: *"Who then is this, that even the wind and the sea obey Him?"* (v. 41). The disciples still have only a cursory understanding of who Jesus really is; therefore, their faith is the size of a bonsai tree instead of an oak.

In contrast, the people Jesus praises for having a "great faith" all seem to "get" who He really is. In Capernaum, a hard-boiled Roman centurion (Matt. 8) humbly asks Jesus to heal his paralytic servant. When Jesus offers to go to the officer's home, the centurion stops him with an answer that is "marvel"-ous: "For I also am a man under authority, with soldiers under me; and I say to this one, 'Go!' and he goes, and to another, 'Come!' and he comes, and to my slave, 'Do this!' and he does it" (v. 9). Jesus, uncharacteristically taken off guard by the man's response, says: "Truly I say to you, I have not found such great faith with anyone in Israel" (v. 10). And this from a pagan invader who, unlike so many of God's "chosen people," understood who Jesus was and acted on that understanding.

Finally, we learn the barefaced truth about the physics of faith from the people in Jesus' hometown: "'Where did this man get this wisdom and these miraculous powers? Is this the carpenter's son? Is not His mother called Mary, and His brothers, James and Joseph and Simon and Judas? And His sisters, are they not all with us? Where then did this man get all these things?' And they took offense at him. But Jesus said to them, 'A prophet is not without honor except in his hometown and in his own household.' And He did not do many miracles there *because of their unbelief*'" (Matt. 13:54–58). It turns out, the dynamics of family and neighborhood and hometown are just as powerfully disruptive in Jesus' life as in our own. The people He grew up around assume they know who He is: "Oh, look, there's that little Jesus who used to live down there on Sarcophagus Street. My, he's grown a big head, hasn't he? Someone should put him in his place." Their truncated faith is directly tied to who they believe Him to be or, to put it another way, to their lack of belief in who He really is. Later, when Jesus is trying to explain to His friends that He's physically going to leave, and that His leaving will be cause for celebration because the Holy Spirit won't come until He's gone and the Holy Spirit is *really something,* He tells them exactly what the third person in the Trinity will be doing when He arrives: "When he comes, he'll expose the error of the godless world's view of sin, righteousness, and judgment: He'll show them that their refusal to believe in me is their basic sin" (John 16:8–9 MSG).

Our refusal to believe in who Jesus is—that's our basic sin. *And our basic sin is the reason why our faith remains stagnant and ineffectual.*

This truth is so crucial to our lives with God that the apostle Paul uses his entire letter to the Galatians as a pretext to defend faith *in Jesus,* rather than faith in a thing (in this case, the law). The turning point in Paul's letter is in chapter 3, verse 25: "But now that faith has come, we are no longer under a tutor." Paul is saying the Old Testament law was only a tutor and is now being replaced by Jesus, who did not come to "abolish" the law but to "fulfill" it. Verse 26 continues: "For you are all sons of God through faith in Christ Jesus." We are made sons when we believe the truth about Jesus, not when we master our ability to wiggle our noses at things.

Paul is writing because the Galatians—who received new life by believing in the grace of Jesus offered to them, not through the law, but *through Him*—are now returning to their old "tutor" instead. And that makes sense because, as we already know, the people of God have for all of history preferred that old "tutor" of the law over the Master Himself. We are frightened and repelled by an actual relationship with God and would prefer to relate to a *thing* rather than to a *Him*. It's a kind of pornography—we'd rather give ourselves to the tantalizing *image* of something we want rather than the messiness of relating to our wife or husband. For men it is photographic images; for women it is the kind of plotlines you find in most romance novels; for the followers of God it is principles, rules, and laws.

And because Paul is no wallflower, he lowers the boom on Peter and those who have followed his lead after Peter returns to the pigsty of his former tutor, the law. Peter does this because some law-living Jews arrive for a visit, take a look around, then criticize him for allowing the community of believers to eschew circumcision. The apostle caves to the pressure of his past and becomes a poser all over again. He returns to the formulas of faith—the outward practice of incantation—and starts requiring that the male Christ followers in his community undergo circumcision. And Paul, ever blunt, blasts him for it—in public.

Paul uses Old Testament Scripture to prove that the law's purpose was to enclose all of us under a curse, so that we who are cursed could receive life and redemption and freedom when that curse was transferred onto the shoulders of God, in Jesus Christ, who paid the price for it. We come under the protective umbrella of that freedom not by more heartily practicing the law under which we're already cursed, the law we have no hope of keeping—but by clinging to the person of Jesus Christ.

Several years ago I lost touch with my friend Chad Arnold after he left our staff and landed at Compassion International, the Colorado-based mercy ministry. About three months ago a mutual friend asked me if I'd heard about what happened to Chad. She told me that in the years since I'd last seen him, Chad's rare liver disease had suddenly grown deadly. He was on the donor list, but it looked as if he might not make it before he advanced to the front of the line. And that's when his younger brother Ryan volunteered to be a "living donor" for Chad. And so Ryan—an athletic, vigorous orthodontist with a wife and three kids—was wheeled into an operating room where surgeons removed 60 percent of his liver to save Chad's life. The operation went well, and Chad's life was dragged back from the brink. But a few days after the operation Ryan suddenly went into cardiac arrest, then descended into a coma. Two days later he was taken off life support and died—the kind of monumental shock no one who knows the brothers will ever get over. Ryan gave his life for Chad, and now Chad must find a way to live his life under the shadow of that sacrifice. For his own part, Chad has committed to honoring the slipstream of his brother's courage and humility. And he has vowed to chronicle his journey in the valley of the shadow of death in an ongoing blog. This morning, this is what he wrote:

> I'd like to say that I would have matured like a fine wine all on my own, if life had played out like it does for most others—calculated, manageable, pseudo-normal. But I don't think so. Truth be told, my world has been turned upside down—and this rodeo isn't over yet.
>
> And I. AM. TIRED.
>
> But mostly I'm tired of hearing myself saying that I'm tired. I'm tired of focusing on MY

experience, MY pain, MY whatever. So I'm not going to do that anymore. Instead, I'm going to just think out loud on paper and let the chips fall where they may. I've been encouraged to write through my pain, but I don't have to keep focusing on it.

So faith. Everyone's got their take.... Seems to me like there are three categories of people as it relates to faith.

1. There are those that believe "If I pray, God answers it according to my desire, and my 'faith' is strengthened as my world remains within my control through my vending-machine God." INSERT PRAYER AND WAIT FOR DESIRED SELECTION. Color me a heretic, but I'm pretty sure that one's been disproved.

2. Then there's the group that has felt the heat of a refining fire but mistaken it for God's wrath. Usually someone in this category is angry, ambivalent, or just plain doesn't believe in a sovereign God, much less a personal one. Maybe their God is themselves. Or a vibe. Or a coconut. I don't know.

3. Then there are those who somehow come crawling out of the ashes and the bedlam—their hair smoking, their clothes smoldering, and their soul blistered. These are people who have prayed heartfelt prayers to a God they've clung to their entire life. Regardless, things didn't turn out like

they planned—not even close. They've got questions, but they're not doubting. They're hurt, but they're not damaged. They're not cracked, but you better believe they are broken. They don't turn their back on God, because in the deepest part of their humanness there is a settling that God is still the only lifeboat left on this fantasy cruise. Not set on understanding, but desperately depending on their only Real Hope.

I think that's the basis of a real, owned faith—and the true purpose of petitioning God. The result of the prayer, really, isn't the point. The lesson learned (or missed) is how we respond—humility and stewardship when we get what we want and total reliance on our Creator when we don't.

You can call that a cop-out. Makes it easy to say you have faith if random is king and anything bad can be explained away as an exercise in personal growth. I'd be lying if I said I could make sense of the context that is now my life. I read some scriptures and the rules don't seem to apply right now. But it's still my choice whether or not I bring my begging bowl back to the feet of God…. I've stopped asking 'Why.' Put anything behind that word—doesn't matter what it is—it's an empty pursuit. I've started asking other things like:

'WHO'—Of the three categories of people, WHO will I choose to be?

'WHAT'—WHAT will define my faith ...
how closely life follows my blueprint?

'WHEN'—WHEN will I become the person
I know I want to be?

'WHERE'—WHERE do I stop and God
begins?...

Never quit the brawl.[4]

Chad's epic story reminds me of something I heard Douglas Wilson say the other day. Wilson, the evangelical pastor who hit the road in 2009 with atheist superstar Christopher Hitchens for a nationwide series of public debates they dubbed *Collision*, responded to Hitchens' declaration that he "sees no role for faith" in life: "Because we're finite, and we all have a limited starting point, it's not a question of whether we have faith; it's what we have faith in. And so, Christopher, I think, has faith in the role of scientific inquiry, rational inquiry. He has faith in that process. And without assuming that process, he can't demonstrate the need for using that process. In short, he has faith or confidence in [rational inquiry]—that it's going to be better than the alternative."[5] Hitchens has placed his faith in what he knows best and trusts most: the seen world. Of course he invests his trust this way—he has no idea who Jesus really is. And as my friend Chad so eloquently points out, many of us in the church have a more kindred relationship with Hitchens than we know.

The Hearing Aid of Faith

In the end, we don't want to hear "puny" and "faith" in the same sentence when the sentence is about us. So how do we grow in the kind of "great faith" Jesus describes? God the Father tries to make it plain for us. In the New Testament we hear the audible voice of God only three times. The second time is on the Mount of Transfiguration, deep into Jesus' public ministry (the first time it happens is just after Jesus comes plunging out of the river Jordan, baptized by His cousin John, and the last time is in John 12, when Jesus asks His Father to glorify His name, and God responds that He already has, and will again). The first two times, the audible voice of His Father booms: "This is my beloved Son, with whom I am well pleased." But the second time—when Peter, James, and John are eyewitnesses to a metaphysical consultation between Jesus, Moses, and Elijah—God's voice interrupts the disciples' fibrillating offer to construct a tabernacle for "The Big Three" by adding an urgent command: *"Listen to Him!"*

Classically, the apostle Paul explains: "Faith comes by hearing, and hearing by the word of Christ" (Rom. 10:17). But the "word of Christ" he's referencing is, of course, the same Jesus that the apostle John describes as he launches into his gospel account: "In the beginning was the Word, and the Word was with God, and the Word was God" (John 1:1). Our faith grows in direct relationship to how often, and how deeply, we listen to Jesus, who is the Word of God. And "listen" transcends what is audible to us—God is bluntly telling us to pay better attention to what Jesus says and does, what He embraces and what He decries, how He responds to both friends and enemies, what He's drawn to and what He's repelled by, what fascinates Him and what bores Him, what is important to Him and what is negligible to Him. Because Jesus is a person and not a map or a principle or a guideline, listening to Him is an everyday art form that requires risk. Canadian singer/songwriter Bruce Cockburn knows this—in "Pacing the Cage" he sings: "Sometimes the best map will not guide you; you can't see what's around the bend. Sometimes the road leads through dark places; sometimes the darkness is your friend."[6] The darkness is our friend because we can't read a map in the dark; we are forced out of necessity to listen to the voice of the Good Shepherd guiding us, to listen instead of choosing our own way. Martin Luther King Jr. was embracing the beauty of the darkness when he said, "Faith is taking the first step, even when you don't see the whole staircase."[7] And we're motivated to take that "first step" because we know who made the stairs, not because we're sure of where they're leading us.

How do we pay better attention to Jesus? John 6 offers us a clue. Jesus has just fed five thousand hungry people by blessing and distributing a few loaves of bread and a few fish; massive crowds are now following Him as if He's the precursor of David Blaine. They want to know how they can get Him to "work the trick" for them, over and over. And Jesus responds: "The work of God is this: to believe in the one he has sent" (v. 29 NIV). Jesus is forcing a turning point in the lives of those who are following Him—He's calling their bluff: "Are you all-in?" He tells them: "This is what my Father wants: that anyone who sees the Son and trusts who he is and what he does and then aligns with him will enter real life, eternal life" (v. 40 MSG). Here He reveals an implicit strategy for growing in our faith:

- *See the Son:* We pay much closer attention to the person of Jesus than to the principles of Jesus. His principles are valuable chiefly because they help

us understand Him, not because we have much
hope of practicing them well. He will practice
His principles *through us* if we'll simply stay connected to Him.

- *Trust in who He is*: Like the centurion, we behave
  as if our knowledge of Jesus is actually true. And
  this trust is in what we know to be true about
  Him, not what we hope He can give to us.

- *Trust in what He does:* We study the things He
  does because they reveal to us how the kingdom
  of God operates—how the Trinity relate to each
  other and, by extension, all the rest of creation.
  This way of relating then becomes our passion,
  because we respect, admire, and are drawn to the
  behavior and the values of the Trinity.

- *Align ourselves with Him:* We give our own
  "blood pledge" to Him, an outward and persistent proclamation—gauged by what we do, not
  what we say—that broadcasts that we're all-in
  with Him.

Our core alignment with Jesus will show up in our habits, not
our rhetoric. A mother needs only her knee-jerk reaction to rescue
her own child from toppling over a wall, but the reaction time can
be a great deal longer (and maybe even too late) if it's someone
else's child. The level of intimacy we enjoy in our various relationships will dictate our behavior in those relationships—whether
we respond in faith or in paralysis. The great philosopher René

Descartes famously said: "I think, therefore I am." We can one-up the Frenchman with this: "I am what I do, not what I think." If we believe the Christian life is primarily about what we think or believe, it's no surprise that so many of us, we must admit, have a tepid relationship with Jesus. Beliefs can be fluid, but a way of life is more like concrete. All of us orbit around a gravitational center in life—Douglas Wilson would call that our "axiomatic starting point." It's whatever we're all-in with. A life spent following Christ is about shifting our all-in to Jesus.

My friend Mike Warden—a life coach, author, and speaker in Austin, Texas—recently blogged about his difficult trip to a screenwriting conference in Los Angeles:

> This was the scene one morning in the skies circling my hotel in L.A. during my recent journey there to take the Story Course with Robert McKee. My first full day in that city had been rough for me—spiritually, emotionally, physically—and the night that followed fared no better. So the next morning I wrestled myself out of bed and took a stroll along the streets bordering my hotel to clear my head and ask God what the heck was going on. Not two seconds after voicing the prayer, I looked up and saw a red-tailed hawk soaring directly overhead with two crows hard on its case, alternately dive-bombing the hawk as it circled the hotel. A voice in my spirit said calmly and with a hint of levity, "That's what's going on."

I continue to be surprised by how slow I can be at times on the uptake about such things. Even Abraham had to fight off the birds to protect the offering God had commanded him to bring. Why should I be so easily surprised by opposition or think of it as something out of the norm? We in the West have been taught that happiness is defined by the absence of such things—resistance, stress, opposition, pressure, suffering, attack. But McKee would argue that true fulfillment, true happiness, cannot exist apart from them.

The logic goes like this: A man longs to find his meaning and purpose in the world. To do that he needs to discover his own true heart—that is, he needs to know what he's made of, who he really is deep inside, whether he is more noble or base … and thereby determine his true place in the world. The thing is, says McKee, the *only* way for him to find out who he really is deep inside is by being forced to make choices under extreme pressure. "You are what you do under pressure," says McKee, "and the greater the pressure, the truer the revelation of who you really are."[8]

We study the stories of Jesus to get closer to the person of Jesus, not to "pattern" ourselves after Him—as if by our will and discipline we could come close to speaking and acting like Jesus. The best use of our energies is not to try harder to be like Jesus, but to stay more closely connected to Him—the branch embedded in the Vine. That means we pay better attention to what He says and does and how others react to Him, simply to get to know Him more deeply. And in knowing Him we see Him better, and in seeing Him better we trust in Him more deeply, and in trusting Him more deeply we align ourselves with Him, and in aligning ourselves with Him we live our lives in a magnetic atmosphere of faith. And that faith, like Peter's, "will not fail."

CHAPTER 6

"AND WHEN YOU HAVE TURNED BACK ..."

(Living under the Promise of God's "When")

I am ready to meet my Maker. Whether my Maker is prepared
for the great ordeal of meeting me is another matter.
—Sir Winston Churchill

The God of the modern evangelical rarely astonishes anybody.
He manages to stay pretty much within the constitution....
He's a very well-behaved God and very denominational and
very much one of us, and we ask Him to help us when we're in
trouble and look to Him to watch over us when we're asleep.
The God of the modern evangelical isn't a God I could have
much respect for. But when the Holy Spirit shows us God as
He is we admire Him to the point of wonder and delight.
—A. W. Tozer, *Worship: The Missing Jewel*

Sometimes you need somebody, if you have somebody to love.
Sometimes you ain't got nobody and you want somebody to love.
Then you don't want to walk and talk about Jesus,
You just want to see His face.
—The Rolling Stones, "Just Want to See His Face"

When I was away from my wife for three months, separated and living
in exile in the basements of friends, I suddenly discovered I was a poet.

I mean, I started writing poems as if it was the most natural thing to do even though I'd had zero interest in poetry prior to my cataclysm. I think the source of this mysterious phenomenon is simple in retrospect—when the walls that you've come to depend upon to keep you safe your whole life are now disintegrating, raining fearsome bricks and debris down on you, you have an unquenchable urge to write poetry.

It's a very dramatic time.

I think people who all of a sudden write poetry fit into one of two categories: either they've entered into a great sorrow, or they've entered into middle school. After *Running the Books* author Avi Steinberg graduated from Harvard he was desperate to find a job that offered dental insurance, so he took a position as the librarian at a tough Boston prison. While there, he helped start a prison poetry club and found many clamoring to join. "There's something about poetry itself that," he says, "somehow fits, as a genre, that fits prison. I don't know what it is.... But there's something about poetry that just gets right to the heart of the matter."[1] I didn't know about this rather unusual side effect of sorrow (and incarceration) because I'd never been kicked out of my house for three months, a cataclysm that forced the discovery that poetry could be a viable emotional relief valve for my despair. I have never written poetry of any kind since those twelve weeks on the rack because, honestly, that time in my life is the closest I've ever come to labor and delivery. And what I gave birth to was poetry. My output was impressive—about one little gem every week, actually. And among those *Cheaper by the Dozen* poem-children, one might be classified as a (minor) epic. I called it, very artistically I thought, "The Greating." It's some sly wordplay between two totally unrelated homonyms—"great" and "grate":

The Greating

Creeping along my heart's cold stone hallway
It is dark, stagnate, foreboding
Dread
There is no outlet, no destination, no self
No hope
Only a vicious grating
Only a vicious greating
Too small for escape
It beckons only to the fool
Near is a
Stone
Rejected by the Builders
Crushing my heart into powder
So it can pour through the greating
Into light
I'd like to get my hands on that Stone
I'd like to get my arms around that Stone
I'd like to rest my head on that Stone
I'd like to swallow that Stone
I'm just desperate enough

Makes you want to invite the Rick-of-yesterday out for a fun evening of miniature golf, or maybe an intervention, right? Whatever the artistic merits of this poem, and I realize there are few, it does perfectly capture the emotional "liminal space"[2] that is the by-product of my seasons of sifting, and all seasons of sifting. You are in confusion and pain and dread and a kind of eager awareness of how miserable you are. You are broken and broken and broken until you almost can't be found. And if you have to be crushed into a powder so you can fit through the grating (or "greating"!) of your dungeon and back out into the light—well, so be it. The operative effect is that your perpetual self-reliance and addictive controlling tendencies are exposed by the beating, then separated from your core identity, thus revealing a *you* that has always been there but has rarely been clearly *seen*. And that *you* is much, much more willing to live dependently—to listen to Jesus and trust Jesus and look to Jesus for your life.

Online one day, searching for a long-forgotten tidbit of something-or-other, I stumbled onto a blog written by banjo-playing Grammy winner Ron Block. Block plays in Alison Krauss's bluegrass band Union Station and is an outspoken Christ follower. In one blog entry, he perfectly captures the dependent momentum our sifting experiences have created in our lives:

> There's a major problem with human effort—
> it doesn't work. The end result of it is either
> self-condemnation or self-righteousness, both
> springing from the same source—false indepen-
> dence from God. The entire history of humanity
> is one of fallen dreams, dashed hopes, unreachable
> utopias. We're not meant to run on our own effort,
> our own vision, our own ways and means of cop-
> ing, because really there is no such thing as human
> independence from God. "He that is not with Me

is against Me." This is an either-or situation. We
are either in union with Christ through dying with
Him on the Cross, or we are still powered by the
mind-set of the "prince of the power of the air, the
spirit that now works in the children of disobedi-
ence." Self-effort or inner reliance on Christ are the
only two options available to us.[3]

In the courtyard of the high priest's home—by the fire, as Peter
warms his hands—"self-effort" and "inner reliance on Christ" are
at war in Peter as he lives out his predicted betrayal. He's unwittingly falling into the sifter. Not far away, Jesus is slapped around
and mocked. And Peter, his eyes now furtive and darting, is quickly
defensive when a few bystanders finger him as a disciple: "Woman,
I do not know Him" (Luke 22:57). His embarrassing denials
quickly build into a ludicrous proclamation: "Man, I do not know
what you are talking about" (v. 60). And the cock crows. And Jesus
turns to look him in the eyes. And Peter disintegrates into tears and
disappears into his own dark night of the soul—he's not there along
the Via Dolorosa to see Jesus drag His cross toward Golgotha. He's
not there when the spikes are nailed into His hands or the spear is
shoved into His side or the veil of the temple is torn in two. He's
not there when Jesus' body is carried into a rich man's tomb, and
he's not there to help roll a massive stone across its entrance. *He's
not there.* But maybe, wherever he's holed up, he feels the shake of
the earthquake when Jesus takes His last breath—the rending of
the earth that trumpets a new earth and a new heaven. In any case,
Peter is like a man buried alive in a mine with only a tiny air pocket

left for his survival, and that air pocket is just this: "When you have turned back."

Jesus and Alfred E. Neuman

What happened there in Peter's "liminal space," where he was buried by the crushing weight of his repeated denials, gasping for air and, likely, plotting his own death? The loss of your identity is the worst thing that can happen to a person—worse than death, if that kind of "worse" can be imagined. People who are thinking of committing suicide know this truth very well; death seems like welcome relief in the face of the obliterating loss of worth and identity. And Peter has lost himself. The cocksure man's man who was the first to name Jesus and the first to defend Him is now exposed as a poser; he has now become a living metaphor for Jesus' blunt warning: "But the one who has heard and has not acted accordingly, is like a man who built a house on the ground without any foundation; and the torrent burst against it and immediately it collapsed, and the ruin of that house was great" (Luke 6:49).

Yes, the ruin of Simon Peter, the Rock of Christ, is great.

And so, the ruined man—the dead man walking—somehow creeps back out of his hole after the resurrection of Jesus and goes back to what once identified him. Peter goes back to the sea, where he has spent so many years as a professional fisherman: "I am going fishing," he says (John 21:3). But he's really saying: "I will fish to find myself again." And we so often do likewise; in the grip of our brokenness and our shame we claw at the "solid me" of our past, like a drowning victim desperate to grasp something that will save him.

I have a good friend who was divorced from his wife after two decades of marriage. For most of his adult life he lived, by sheer force of his will to succeed, in a marriage that was slowly dismantling him, piece by piece. She'd had several affairs, but he vowed he would never divorce her—that he would rather die than give up on his marriage. And in the end he, like Peter, had to swallow the bitterness of a shattered relationship. There was not much remaining of my friend in the wake of this catastrophic loss of his identity. He, like Peter, disappeared and crawled into a hole. I asked him to describe his long journey in the liminal space, penned in by the wallpaper of shame and failure:

> I ran from God and went back to what I knew to do—running [a small retreat and conference center]. I felt like I was a worm. A guy came in and asked if I was the janitor. I embraced that identity because I wanted to be hidden. This was "going back to fishing" for me. I spent ten years fishing, there at [the retreat center]. And there was another couple who worked there—they were the overseers for the young people who lived there as residents. Once, before they left for a two-week break, we talked about ways we could recruit residents who were healthier and had more to contribute to the ministry. As part of that pursuit, while this couple was away, we started a dialogue with a ministry that could feed us young leaders. When the couple came back they found out about this dialogue and burst

into my office, screaming at me—they called me a liar. So I arranged for us to meet with the founders of [the retreat center] to talk it all out. In that meeting this couple asked the founders to let me go and recommended themselves as my replacements. The man who cofounded the center listened patiently and then told them, "Actually, you're out." The couple's reaction was total disbelief.

In my mind I can imagine Jesus saying to Satan: "I want you to go down and sift that place." Why would He do that? Well, to get me out of my fishing boat. I had to take over all of the young people who were there, because we didn't replace the couple who'd been overseeing our residents. That's when I began to get my swing back, because that's what I was created to be and do—pour myself into young people, surfacing who they are in Christ. In the wake of my great shame I was elusive—I didn't own my game because I had lost myself. This was the beginning of my journey toward being "impressed" with the Lord, of the time of my close connection to the Lord. I was using the gifts He'd given me to use—I was revived, restored, and reinstated. My ten years of fishing was fueled by shame and failure, so my friends prayed for me and broke the power of that shame in me. Like Elrond confronting Aragorn in *The Lord of the Rings*, God asked me to "put aside the Ranger" and become who I was meant to be.[4]

Jesus understands that we will "go back to fishing" under the pressure and destruction of our sifting; He also knows that we, like Peter and my friend, are created to be more than that. We've been redeemed and set free to be *fishers of men*. When Jesus casually speaks hope into Peter's coming darkness—"And when you turn back"—the "you" is once again singular, not plural. He is speaking directly to Peter, not to the "you" of the disciples gathered in that upper room. And when we are in the midst of our sifting, we need Jesus to speak directly to us. We crave His singular voice speaking into our singular darkness. Jesus is not *hoping* Peter will come back from the edge—it's not a "wish upon a star." *He is telling him that he will turn back—that he will survive his sifting.*

When my wife has her monthly infusion treatments, she schedules them for the days I'm working at home because she wants me to hold her hand when Kathy the nurse sticks the IV needle in her hand or wrist or forearm. Because of her ongoing health issues, Bev has been stuck countless times with an IV needle. Some of those experiences, mostly with Kathy, have been quick and relatively painless—and some have been horrendous and frightening. Getting stuck with a needle is a microexperience of sifting for most people—just ask any child why she fears going to the doctor. My hand in Bev's hand says, *You will get to the other side of this—this will be over soon, and I'm here with you now.* And then the needle is inside the vein, taped down and quickly attached to the plastic tubing that allows immunoglobulin to be pumped into her system. She doesn't need my hand now—but she needed it *then,* at the moment the pain entered her body.

When Jesus tells Peter he will survive his sifting, it is a great kindness—a hand holding his hand. He is trying to tell His beloved friend that He is not worried about him, that despite the loneliness and horror Peter is about to descend into, he will see the light of day again. And, likewise, Jesus is right now *not worried about you and me.* He is relaxed about your future, no matter how much your future sometimes resembles a cesspool. Picture the ugly mug of Alfred E. Neuman on the cover of *Mad* with the iconic "What, me worry?" over his head. It stretches the boundaries of credulity, but this is Jesus. We have not yet "turned back," but the faith of Jesus asserts that we will. He is relaxed and confident about this. It would be hard to have greater faith than Jesus has, and this is our hope. He is already nurturing a life for us on the other side of our darkness (John 14:2), preparing the soil for beauty to rise again. In the title song of Steven Curtis Chapman's *Beauty Will Rise* album (explored at greater length in chapter 1), the singer/songwriter beautifully describes how the sifted, separated, and revealed respond when they hear Jesus say "and when you have turned back":

> *But buried deep beneath all our broken dreams*
> *We have this hope:*
> *Out of these ashes ... beauty will rise*
> *And we will dance among the ruins*
> *We will see Him with our own eyes*[5]

After his third denunciation of Jesus in the high priest's court-yard Peter "went out and wept bitterly" (Luke 22:62). His remorse mirrors the suicidal grief of Judas, who despairs of what he's done and begs the stone-faced Pharisees to take back the thirty silver pieces he was paid, finally throwing his blood money at their feet. But

Judas's sorrow and shame differ from Peter's in at least one crucial respect: Judas believes the voice of the Enemy—that his true identity is that of a betrayer, a poser, a nothing. Suicide is not such a radical decision when you've already determined the *you* that you've always seen yourself to be is now a nothing, a vapor that only hints at the person who was once a solid. Would God's purposes still have been completed had Judas repented after his betrayal and turned back to Jesus? Yes. In God's redemption scheme, someone was going to betray Jesus to the Jewish leaders—Judas did that after "Satan then entered into him" (John 13:27). The plan does not require the death of the betrayer, any more than Adam and Eve's betrayal required their death or our betrayal seals our death warrant. But the story of Judas is heartbreaking and distinct in comparison to Peter's refusal to take his own life and his choice to, instead, journey through his sifting. Peter falls on the "Cornerstone" and is broken to pieces, while the stone falls on Judas and he is crushed (Matt. 21:44).

I've mentioned that John Newton wrote "Amazing Grace" more than two centuries ago to celebrate the fruit of his sifting—honoring God for rescuing him from a sordid life as a slave-ship captain. He'd spent much of his adult life herding frightened, desperate Africans into the hell of his ship's hold, then selling those who survived the perilous crossing of the Atlantic to wealthy landowners in America. So, when Newton penned "saved a wretch like me," he wasn't kidding. If you look up the song in the Library of Congress you'll see that the words were written by Newton but the melody is ascribed to "Unknown." That's because, according to gospel artist Wintley Phipps, Newton likely first heard the original melody for the song embedded in one of the West African laments he heard repeatedly wafting up from the hold of his ship, where the terrified slaves below sang their prayers to God. In "Amazing Grace," Newton identifies himself with the hopeless victims who'd been sifted by his heartless actions.[6] And in the grief of his own "dark night of the soul," when he was buried in the mine shaft of his own shame, Newton understood the deeper meaning locked up in "amazing" and "grace." In his song he is refreshingly desperate.

Contrast the first time Newton sang this hymn—alone, perhaps—with the way you and I have typically sung it in church. How many of us *really* identify ourselves as "wretches" when we sing the familiar chorus? Do we need God's grace as much as Newton's barefaced confession shows he did? More likely, if we were to translate Newton's lyrics to accurately reflect how we often stand outside of the song, we would sing: "Expected grace, how innocuous the sound, that gave a friendly nudge to a pretty good guy like me." This is no great revelation—those of us in the Western world live in the most affluent, excessive culture in the history of the earth. In the United States, when we're living our "American dream," we're in no surface danger of want. So why make believe we're thirsty for God's grace when we're not really all that thirsty? Only sifting has the power to parch our souls—to create the saving thirst that we can never produce on our own. I heard Steve Fitzhugh, a former professional football player who now directs an inner-city ministry in Washington, DC, describe a speaking trip to Zimbabwe, where a local pastor said to him, "Steve, in America you believe in God. In Africa, we depend on God."[7]

The gruff and gravel-voiced singer/songwriter Tom Waits perfectly captures this parching of the soul—the painful contrasts that produce a thirsty dependence, leading us to God's grace—in his song "San Diego Serenade":

> *I never saw the morning till I stayed up all night*
> *I never saw the sunshine till you turned out the light....*
> *I never saw the East Coast till I moved to the West....*
> *I never saw your heart until someone tried*
> *to steal, tried to steal it away*
> *I never saw your tears until they rolled down your face*[8]

Until we have lost what we've taken for granted, we can't really see its true value. And until Peter loses himself in the courtyard of the high priest, he has no idea how precarious his attachment to Jesus is—"I never saw You, Jesus, until I betrayed You." And he doesn't truly realize that his identity has been built on shifting sand. How could a man like Peter arrive at this kind of understanding apart from an experience that has the leverage to separate him from his false identity? In the wake of Jesus' revelation to Peter that he is going to be sifted and that he will turn back from his betrayal and find himself again, the do-and-do-and-do fisherman is positively incredulous: "Lord, with You I am ready to go both to prison and to death!" It's likely that "when you turn back" infuriates Peter in this moment—Jesus' matter-of-fact statement of hope adds to the offensiveness of what He's said because He sounds so *certain* that Peter is about to do the unthinkable. And it's that certainty, coming from his beloved Jesus, that feels like a betrayal to Peter. In effect, his response back to Him is akin to saying: *"Nobody says 'when you turn back' to me!*

How dare You suggest that I'm the kind of man who would abandon and betray his best Friend and Rabbi! I've never offered anything less than my life for my friends!" The pain of what Jesus has said to him reverberates as he stands there warming his hands in the high priest's courtyard—he has translated the warning into an indictment, and he's furious that his years of close friendship and costly service seem to have lost their currency. Earlier, in the garden of Gethsemane, Peter tries to defend Jesus by pulling his sword and cutting off the ear of Malchus, the high priest's slave. He is trying to make his point: *"There will be no 'turning back,' because I'm going down swinging. You're wrong about me, Jesus. You're wrong."*

In medical terms, Peter is angry at his doctor's diagnosis, and he's decided to fight back by proving Him wrong. But this is no quack— Jesus is not fooling around. It's in these moments that the "Doctor" seems immovably dedicated to telling the truth about our condition: "I never lie, but I am a savage." The brick wall of His assessment is something we have to smash into repeatedly, then finally acknowledge, before we can even hear the tender love behind His "when you turn back." You could call it denial, or you could call it a stubborn resistance to embrace the truth about who we are, or you could call it fear. In any case, we do not easily swallow the promise that things are going to get worse before they get better, and that we are as needy and as lost as Jesus says we are.

Right now as I write, I'm sitting in a room next to the surgical area where a skin surgeon has just removed squamous-cell cancer from my right cheekbone. In a week I have to come back to this place and have an identical cancer removed from my left cheekbone. Prior to the surgery, sitting in a reclinable dentist's chair, surrounded by trays of surgical instruments that are covered by towels to keep people like me from freaking out, I listened to the doctor casually describe what he was about to do with a needle and a scraper (that he compared to a melon scoop) and a scalpel. I was a scared little boy again, wringing my hands and feeling all alone. And more than that, I was well aware that these cancers could've been prevented had I come in for my regular six-month treatment.

Because I'm whiter than Casper the Friendly Ghost, the sun has been my enemy for most of my life—the time-delayed fruit of a really bad burn when I was a teenager is a face-full of precancerous lesions that can be easily held in check if I'll just show up for my chemical peel twice a year. Doctors created the term *chemical peel* to divert our attention from a more literal description of the procedure, which is "an acid bath for the face." Because I told myself, every month, that I was too busy that month to have my face bathed in acid, and because I told myself that lie for more than a year, two cancers had time to develop on my face. Now I have to have them cut out, and I'll have two pirate scars on either side of my face. Maybe I can follow Jesus' advice and pluck out one of my eyes, just to finish off the look with a black patch.

The point is that I'm very aware of what I did to get myself to this place, but I haven't had to face the full consequences of that truth until now, with a bright light shining on my face and a guy with a knife hovering over me. The truth of my situation is, right now, immovable. And I wish I hadn't told my wife to stay home from my appointment because it would be "no big deal." It's not a big deal, of course, until you're paying the piper and the pain sets in. And when Peter runs from the high priest's courtyard, shattered and lost, the truth of Jesus' diagnosis is inescapable and immovable—the bright light of the truth reveals much that is ugly in our souls, and we wrestle with despair expressly because control has been taken from us. Only now does Jesus' promise of "when you turn back" even matter to Peter—and now that it matters to him, it is the *only* thing that really matters to him. He is now parched for Jesus—hungry enough and thirsty enough for Him that His offensive "eat My body and drink My blood" is no longer so far-fetched. He wants Jesus because He needs Jesus—he is moving from mere belief to dependency. Or, more deeply true, he is moving from application to attachment.

Application versus Attachment

I've now clocked more than two decades as a magazine editor, applying my own sifting process to thousands of articles and dozens of books. Among other perks, editing the opinions and ideas of so many has served up broad insights into the prevalent and expected ways we Christians think about our lives with God. And for a long time a certain maxim subconsciously embedded in almost every Bible study, curriculum, or "spiritual growth" idea I've ever seen has really bothered me. It's a prevalent formula for discipleship that bubbles to the surface over and over. Recently, during my long, slow crawl through 156 lessons of a small-group curriculum for senior highers, I finally understood the formula well enough to name it:

Understand the biblical principle, then apply it to your life.

Wow, what a dramatic buildup for something that seems positively innocuous, right? It's just a dolphin fin breaking the surface of the ocean—until you look a little closer and realize that it's a shark, not a dolphin, out there. This ubiquitous, suprarational, linear,

I'm-in-control philosophy is not only suspect as a results-proven discipleship strategy, it's not even all that biblical.

First, "understand and apply" implies that greater knowledge will lead to our transformation. That's not biblically or experientially all true. Satan *understands* the Bible enough to debate it with Jesus in the wilderness (Matt. 4:1–11)—but he was not transformed by his understanding. Likewise, I understand the concept of sin, but that hasn't kept me from sinning. And every married couple on their wedding day understands the basics of how marriage is supposed to work, but that doesn't mean they're going to stay married. Understanding is important, but it isn't the same as transformation.

Second, the whole understand-and-apply formula is based on our ability to somehow transfer understood truths to the core of who we are. But what exactly does "apply it to my life" look like, and is it anything like painting my house? The "application" mantra seems to promise that we can simply slap some truth-shellac on our souls and get it to stick. It follows that people who aren't all that transformed must be pretty pathetic housepainters, metaphorically speaking. They just don't *get* this transformation-by-application thing—but, really, does anyone *get it* all that well? Once, on a workplace leadership retreat, I asked everyone to turn to a partner and share a truth about the Christian life that they'd learned over their lifetime. After a few minutes of discussion, I asked the pairs to come up with some way to apply that truth to their lives in the next few minutes. This turned out to be a really, really hard thing to do—even for people who are "professional Christians." We might understand the biblical principle of "reaping what you sow," but what would you do, right now, to "apply it to your life"? That takes a lot of thought and discipline and perseverance and creativity, and even then the results will be mixed.

Application as a discipleship strategy is severely overrated—real transformation happens when we draw near to God, because He's the only One who can really change us. Paul, in his letter to the Christians in Philippi, declares, "We're waiting the arrival of the Savior, the Master, Jesus Christ, who will ... make us beautiful and whole with the same powerful skill by which he is putting everything as it should be, under and around him" (Phil. 3:20–21 MSG). We need transformation, not incremental improvement. That's exactly why Jesus primarily defined discipleship and growth in *botanical* terms—He told us that we're dying branches in desperate need of *attaching ourselves* to a growing Vine, and the Vine is Jesus Himself (John 15; Rom. 11). Remember, when Jesus chooses a metaphor to explain the inexplicable, He always chooses the *perfect* metaphor. Dying-branch-now-connected-to-living-Vine perfectly describes what discipleship actually looks like. Get closer to Jesus, and His life will start to spill into your veins—and that life will literally transform you, and your transformation will produce fruit, which will look a lot like the fruit of the Spirit, the same stuff that we've been told to "apply to our lives."

In the application version of discipleship, we're supposed to grab (understand) what fruit we can and sort of duct-tape it (apply it) to our souls. In contrast, when we see ourselves as branches and focus our lives on becoming more attached to the Vine, we naturally produce fruit because of who we're attached to. And we become more deeply attached to Him, ironically, by *understanding Him* for who He really is (not understanding-and-applying His principles better). In his book *Following Jesus,* the great British pastor and theologian N. T. Wright says, "The longer you look at Jesus, the more you will want to serve him. That is of course, if it's the real Jesus you're looking at."[9] Wright says that it's very possible for us to miss the "real Jesus"—that we can literally forget who He *really* is. This is why Paul, in his introductory remarks to the Philippians, says he's praying something very specific on their behalf: "that your love may abound still more and more in real knowledge and all discernment" (1:9). To what end is he praying that the Philippians will apply this "real knowledge and all discernment"? Well, to the person of Jesus Christ—that their love for Him will "abound still more and more." In 1 Corinthians 2:2 the "Pharisee of Pharisees," one of the most learned men of his day, reduces himself to this: "For I am determined to know nothing among you except Jesus Christ, and Him crucified." And later in the New Testament, our man Peter underscores the passionate focus of our understanding: "grow in the grace and knowledge of our Lord and Savior Jesus Christ" (2 Peter 3:18).

Understand-and-apply is a me-centered, exhausting, and ultimately demoralizing exercise in manufactured grace. It is the same exercise once practiced by the Pharisees, who were lambasted over and over by Jesus for practicing a "form of religion" without its "substance." We cling to it because we are controlling—we understand how to do-and-do-and-do but, as I've said, we don't understand how to abide.

Application can take us only so far. Sifting will expose it for what it often really is—a willful determination to live our lives outside of desperate dependency on the grace of God. It is the passionate pursuit of "self-effort" as a substitute for "inner reliance on Christ," to use Ron Block's comparison. This substitution is perfectly portrayed in the Oscar-winning film *Good Will Hunting*, the story of a troubled young genius named Will Hunting who, as he moves through life, relates to the people around him with rage and cocksure arrogance, leaving a trail of wrecked relationships and grief in his wake. He's a walking illustration of a psychological truism: "Hurt people hurt people." His quick wit and pseudointellectual arguments create a kind of magnetism that he leverages to brutalize and betray everyone who tries to get close to him. All of that changes when he's forced to meet with a psychologist named Sean Maguire—a broken man whose wife has recently died after a long battle with cancer. After a particularly disturbing interchange, when Will disparages the psychologist's dead wife, the two meet for their next session at a park bench. Sean, played by Robin Williams, lowers the boom on Will, played by Matt Damon:

> Sean: Thought about what you said to me the other day.... Stayed up half the night thinking about it. Something occurred to me ... fell into a deep peaceful sleep, and haven't thought about you since. Do you know what occurred to me?

> Will: No.

> Sean: You're just a boy. You don't have the faintest idea what you're talking about.

Will: Why, thank you.

Sean: It's all right. You've never been out of Boston.

Will: No.

Sean: So if I asked you about art you could give me the skinny on every art book ever written. Michelangelo, you know a lot about him. Life's work, political aspirations, ... the whole works, right? But I'll bet you can't tell me what it smells like in the Sistine Chapel. You've never actually stood there and looked up at that beautiful ceiling. If I ask you about women, you'd probably give me a syllabus about your personal favorites.... But you can't tell me what it feels like to wake up next to a woman and feel truly happy.... And I'd ask you about war, you'd probably throw Shakespeare at me, right? "Once more unto the breach, dear friends." But you've never been near one. You've never held your best friend's head in your lap, watch him gasp his last breath looking to you for help. I'd ask you about love, you'd probably quote me a sonnet. But you've never looked at a woman and been totally vulnerable. Known someone that could level you with her eyes, feeling like God put an angel on earth just for you.... And you wouldn't know what it's like to be her angel, to have that love for her, be there forever, through anything, through cancer. And you wouldn't know about sleeping sitting up in the hospital room for two months, holding her hand, because the doctors could see in your eyes that the terms "visiting hours" don't apply to you. You don't know about real loss, 'cause it only occurs when you've loved something more than you love yourself. And I doubt you've ever dared to love anybody that much.[10]

Will has understood true things, and he's applied true things, but he's not *attached* to true things. He's living out of the shell of his identity but doesn't know it until an aging, broken man gives him the greatest gift of his life—he sifts him. And this is exactly the place where Peter stands just before the cock crows and Jesus turns to look at him. He has listened to Jesus and tried to apply what he's heard, but he's about to discover that he's not intimately attached to Jesus ... yet. Spurgeon describes the scene:

> What a sight it must have been for Peter! Our dear Master's face was that night all red from the bloody sweat. He must have appeared emaciated in body; His eyes weary with want of sleep, and His whole countenance the vision of grief. If ever a picture of the Man of Sorrows could have been drawn, it should have been taken at that moment when the Lord turned and looked upon Peter. By torchlight and the flickering flame of the fire in

the court of the hall of Caiaphas Peter saw a vision which would never fade from his mind. He saw the man whom he loved as he had never seen Him before.[11]

And it's also true that Peter sees himself as he has never seen himself before—Clint Eastwood is firing blanks. He's been emptied of his arrogance and self-reliance. In that moment he is broken and broken and broken. And though the break is akin to surgery without anesthesia, this separation from his former identity breaks open a wound that will allow him to be *grafted into the Vine,* who is Jesus. In Romans 11 Paul goes into great detail to explain this metaphor of grafting—we are like branches that have been attached to a family of sin that tracks back to Adam and Eve, and when we offer ourselves to Jesus He reaches out and snaps us off from our poisonous past. Now we have an open, gaping wound and will surely die unless we are grafted in to a healthy Vine. My wife and I visited a local nursery to ask an expert there to explain the process of grafting to us. The comparisons to our own lives with Christ were so profound that worship bubbled over in us. To graft, you must first clip a branch from a weak and poorly producing tree and shear off its leaves. Then you use a sharp knife to create a point on the end of the graft before splitting the root stalk of a healthy plant right down the middle. Finally, into the open wound of the root stalk, you shove the pointed end of the graft stalk and wrap the whole thing with thick tape to keep it in place. Months later you can unwrap the graft—the ugly wound still readily apparent—to reveal a death-sentence branch that is now alive because of the life flowing into it from the root.

These are the basics of grafting. But it's one thing to understand the concept; it's quite another to watch it happen through the lens of your own journey with Christ. Grafting, like our own attachment to Christ, is a casually violent process. In the comparison, *we are the grafted branch*—and if that branch had a soul (and we do) it would be certain it was about to die. We know too well the snip-snip of our "leaves" and the unbearable severing from our toxic sources of life. And even after our graft is secured, the wound is obvious and often ugly looking. We will never escape the outward evidence of our wounds, even though we will thrive as never before because of them. But a graft is impossible unless the root stalk is also cut, right down its tender middle. Without a gaping wound in both the grafted branch (us) and the root (Jesus) it would be impossible to secure an organic and permanent attachment (our salvation) to God. Of course, we know all about the pain of our own wounds, but when was Jesus "split down the middle"? Of course, it happened on the cross, but the moment can be pinpointed further: It is when Jesus screams, "My God, My God, why have You forsaken Me?" (Mark 15:34). Now the One who has never known anything other than intimacy with His Father and the Spirit, whose infinite beginning and infinite end are framed by an unconditionally loving community, is more alone than anyone has ever been or ever will be. A forsaken Jesus is an entirely *other* experience than a forsaken *you* or *me*.

In the garden and in our lives with God, the goal of grafting is intimacy, not behavior change. And intimacy with God produces nourishing fruit. When we are grafted—*attached to Jesus*—we produce an abundance of fruit that looks and tastes like the Vine but is unique to our particular "graft." Fruit from a grafted tree is of much higher quality than the original, and it is produced much faster (one to two years instead of six to seven years).

Jesus says, in John 15: "Abide in Me, and I in you. As the branch cannot bear fruit of itself unless it abides in the vine, so neither *can* you unless you abide in Me" (v. 4). The italics here are already in the text; I didn't add them. We simply cannot—*cannot*—bear fruit by ourselves. No matter how hard we're working to produce it by understanding and applying, those efforts will be thwarted and undermined, whether from our utter inability to summon the kind of perfect discipline understanding and applying require to succeed, or because our willful efforts are quickly exposed under the bright light of our sifting. The application path produces fruit that looks legitimate for a time and from a distance. But sooner or later someone will get close enough to your fruit to see that it's held on by duct tape—and that it's starting to rot. Jesus, ever gentle and kind, will not let His brothers and sisters live their lives in the midst of rotting fruit. He will knock that fake fruit off our branches, then invite us to abide. And this, again, is the great problem—for do-and-do-and-do people like Peter and like us, *abide* is an inscrutable word. How do you apply *abide?* Jesus' invitation is not a call from the boss to up our production; it's a call from our Lover, who wants us to come to bed. Our lives are really about drawing ever nearer to Jesus, the source of "living water"—not trying ever harder to be a better Christian.

Though we most often are blind to it, the application mantra is attractive because, essentially, we can practice it without a desperate dependence on the Vine. We don't have to actually be in relationship with Jesus to study His truths and apply them. That's attractive to us because we're fundamentally dedicated to staying in control, and relationships work against control. We can understand the principles of Jesus and stay in control, but when we relate to Him we discover that He is, of course, an "untamed lion." He will say and do things that surprise us—actually, "shock" is more like it. In a lecture entitled "The Shocking Beauty of Jesus," C. S. Lewis scholar Dr. Peter Kreeft told a class of Boston University students:

> Christ changed every human being He ever met.... If anyone claims to have met Him without being changed, he has not met Him at all. When you touch Him, you touch lightening.... I think Jesus is the only man in history who never bored anyone. I think this an empirical fact, not just a truth of faith. It's one of the reasons for believing His central claim, and Christianity's central claim, that He is literally God in the flesh....
>
> The Greek word used to describe everyone's reaction to Him in the Gospels is *thauma*—wonder. This was true of His enemies, who killed Him. Of His disciples, who worshiped Him. And even of agnostics, who went away shaking their heads and muttering, "No man ever spoke like this man," and knowing that if He didn't stop being what He was and saying what He said that eventually they would have to side with either His killers or His worshippers. For "Jesus shock" breaks your heart in two and forces you to choose which half of your heart you will follow.[12]

Our apply-the-principles mentality is subconsciously designed to remove surprise and shock from our Christian life—to make the whole thing more like software that we download and less like a marriage, which, as you know, requires incredible courage in the face of exposure and heartbreak. We somehow sense, as Kreeft says, that a true attachment to Him will certainly *change* us. And most of us, unremarkably, prefer the hell we know to the change we don't know. Our reluctance to enter into relationship with God, preferring instead to understand and apply, is exactly the sin of the Pharisees. No one understood God's law better, and no one spent more time and energy thinking through how to apply these laws into every conceivable situation—they made a cottage industry out of it: "Once, having been asked by the Pharisees when the kingdom of God would come, Jesus replied, 'The kingdom of God does not come with your careful observation, nor will people say, "Here it is," or "There it is," because the kingdom of God is within you'" (Luke 17:20–21 NIV).

We do not enter into the kingdom of God by "careful observation" of God's principles—the kingdom is not something outside of us that we apply to our lives. It is the lifeblood of the Vine, and only the grafted-in branches share in it. Jesus assesses the Pharisees' application mentality this way: "Woe to you! For you are like concealed tombs, and the people who walk over them are unaware of it" (Luke 11:44). There is death concealed in our application strategies. There is life waiting for us when we move toward attachment instead. And this is what Peter is about to experience, as his tears come and come and come, and as he reemerges from his dark hiding place into the blinding light of the resurrection.

Naked and Unashamed

In John 21, the "disciple whom Jesus loved" records a stunning scene on the shores of the Sea of Tiberias. Here, after the resurrection of Jesus, a restless Peter who's been separated from his identity and not yet reunited with his Master and Friend tells the other disciples that he's going to go fishing; six of them decide to join him, fishing all night and catching nothing. At daybreak they see the figure of a man on the shore, calling to them: "Children, you do not have any fish, do you?" And of course, they do not. So the man on the shore calls out to them, telling them to cast their net on the right side of the boat—"and then they were not able to haul it in because of the great number of fish" (v. 6). As they are fighting to bring the catch into the boat John turns excitedly to Peter, points to the shore, and says: "It is the Lord" (v. 7). And Peter scrunches up his eyes to discern the man on the shore and then explodes—*just explodes*—with desire. He's stripped naked for work, but he must get to Jesus NOW. So he quickly ties his garment around his waist and, like a child rushing to meet his soldier daddy who's home from the war, plunges into the choppy waters and swims furiously to shore. The boat follows behind as Peter thrashes his way to Jesus, who is calmly building a fire so they can have breakfast together.

When Simon Peter arrives onshore, panting and naked and dripping wet, he stands before Jesus. In the garden, before the fall, Adam and Eve stood before God "naked and unashamed." Now Peter— *beaten, separated, and revealed*—stands again before God, naked and unashamed. Maybe he's the first person since the great fall to do it. The distance and self-consciousness that sin and betrayal creates is obliterated in the passion of his reunion. And this is our story too.

On the other side of our nightmare, on the other side of our sifting, Jesus invites us to come back to Him. And for some of us that invitation will be the first time we've ever given our whole heart to Jesus. We will stand before Him naked, dripping wet and disheveled, unaware of our nakedness, our eyes fixed on Him and a smile terrorizing the memory of our pain. And our whole world is waiting there in His eyes—our lives from that moment will be all about getting near to Jesus, treasuring every moment with Him, seeing Him with new eyes and hearing Him with new ears. From now on, we will taste and see that He is good (Ps. 34:8). We will be freer than we've ever been before.

There, standing before the resurrected Jesus on the shore, Peter feels none of the shame of his sifting. None of the cowardly behavior. None of the fury and defensiveness. None of the emptiness and the recrimination. There is only the kind of raw longing that is so powerful and magnetic in a man. Nothing, not even the comfort of his self-reliance and his carefully cultivated persona, matters now. Only Jesus matters.

Five or six years ago I was invited to speak at a large youth ministry conference in the Midwest. The organizers wanted me to offer something a little deeper for those who were ready for a different approach to ministry, so they gave me a two-hour preconference slot and the freedom to do whatever I wanted to do. At the time, I was experimenting with a training idea that focused all of ministry on three vital questions:

"Who do I say Jesus is?"
"Who does Jesus say I am?"
"Who do I say I am?"

When I emerged from that two-hour training session I felt like Peter on the shore of the Sea of Tiberias—I was full of hunger for Jesus. A workshop at a youth ministry conference had morphed into one of the most powerful worship experiences of my adult life. We had pursued Jesus not to learn how to apply His principles, but to enjoy Him. And because it was a preconference slot, I had the freedom to explore the rest of the event as an attendee—the perfect setup for me on the heels of my experience with Jesus. I had no responsibilities and lots to tempt my curiosity. So I went to every general session and popped in to many workshops. I listened to some of the best ministry speakers in the world, all of them experts in what you might call the "tips and techniques" of the application mentality. And in the middle of what I would normally expect to be an invigorating experience, I quickly realized my soul was being invaded by a pervading sense of dissonance. I was restless and, I had to admit, absolutely bored by almost everything I was hearing. I knew in my head that the strategies they were dispensing "worked." But the more I listened the less interested I was in stuff that "works."

Disillusioned and suddenly feeling disconnected from the very people I've always relished, I found an empty seat in the cavernous atrium just outside the main session's doors. Thousands of people were buzzing around me, chatting and hurrying along to their next application download, but I felt utterly alone among them. Finally, I closed my eyes and whispered aloud: "Why, why, why, Jesus, am I feeling this way?" Tears rolled down my cheeks. I was desperate to understand what was happening inside me. And into that liminal space I heard His voice, unmistakably whispering back to me: *"You're bored by everything but Me now."*

And then the little streams of my tears joined the Mississippi, and I quietly sobbed in my chair. *You're bored by everything but Me now.* I knew it was true. The tips and techniques of an application mentality seemed like ridiculous distractions from the attachment I craved. I sat there crying, naked and unashamed. The truth of Jesus' love for me, and the very magnetic effect of His nearness, washed over me. And I opened my mouth to drink it in—to drink Him in. I was desperately thirsty for Him, to eat His body and drink His blood. And I know, I just know, that this is what Peter felt as he thrashed his way to shore and stood there naked before Jesus. The separation of boat and water were unconscionable barriers to his thirst, which his Master and Lover Jesus soon quenched with the same offer He made to the woman at the well in John 4:

> Everyone who drinks of this water will thirst again; but whoever drinks of the water that I will give him shall never thirst; but the water that I will give him will become in him a well of water springing up to eternal life. (vv. 13–14)

And is our response, like the woman's, full of innocence and yearning? "Sir, give me this water, so I will not be thirsty" (v. 15)? If you've been beaten and separated and revealed, you know exactly what she was longing for.

CHAPTER 7

"STRENGTHEN YOUR BROTHERS."

(Discovering That You Have Something Great to Give)

It seemed to me that among his achievements, great as they were, his one failure was the most glorious. We have pierced the veneer of outside things. We have suffered, starved, and triumphed. Groveled down, but grasped at glory. Grown bigger in the bigness of the whole. We have seen God in His splendors, heard the text that nature renders. We had reached the naked soul of man.

—Frank Worsley, former captain of the *Endurance*, on the legacy of Sir Ernest Shackleton upon his death.

Life can only be understood backwards;
but it must be lived forwards.

—Søren Kierkegaard

Alas, how easily things go wrong!
A sigh too much, or a kiss too long,
And there follows a mist and a weeping rain,
And life is never the same again....
But what is left for the cold, gray soul,
That moans like a wounded dove?
One wine is left in the broken bowl—
'Tis—to love, and love, and love.

—George MacDonald, from *Phantastes*

A couple of years ago I had a dream—one of those deep-of-the-night visions that's so vivid it's hard to believe it didn't really happen. In the dream I saw myself standing self-consciously on a vast prairie, on the crest of a windswept hill. I was dwarfed by a small throng of mounted horsemen, all of whom looked and sounded and smelled like men well acquainted with terrible and epic adventures. They were scarred and rough and relaxed in the saddle—they had the look of men who could be counted on, no matter what was thrown their way. Looking around I was startled to see Jesus among them—mounted and tall astride a horse fidgeting with excitement and ready to plunge down the hill at his master's first nudge. And in my dream Jesus leaned over, smiling, with His hand outstretched, beckoning—I could smell the earthy mix of leather and sweat on Him. And His eyes flashed with delight as He said:

"Mount up, son. I want you to ride with Me."

And right then one of His men appeared, leading a riderless horse to me. Embarrassed and eager I grabbed the reins and the horn of the saddle and swung myself awkwardly onto the horse's back, my feet not quite reaching the stirrups. And suddenly there was a wink and a whistle and a shout, and a great cloud of dust kicked up as the entire party wheeled off and charged down the hill into the great unknown. And I kicked at my horse and winced as the saddle slapped my butt with the force of a car wreck and the wind blew my hair back while I did everything I could to hang on. And I smiled through my gritted teeth, eyes flashing like a boy about to ski off the lift for the first time in his life.

After the dream I awoke, suddenly, with my heart pumping and tears streaming down my face. I was breathing hard and trying to find my bearings. I wondered, *Was this a true invitation or merely the confluence of all my deepest hopes?* In reality it doesn't matter, because the dream reveals my soul's true bent. More fundamental than anything else in my life, and more compelling than all lesser pursuits, I long to be invited into the small scouting party of His grafted-in brothers and sisters whose only passion is to stay close to Jesus—to join Him in His passion and purpose to "free the [beloved] captives" (Isa. 42:7 NLT). If we "ride" with Him, the adventure will take us into forbidding landscapes, and we will know the deepest joy our hearts can experience: It's the certainty that our own Beloved has sacrificed everything to reclaim us and is depending on us to give what we have to give in service to His great Cause ("For the Son of Man came to seek and to save what was lost" [Luke 19:10 NIV]). This, in the end, is what fuels the reckless behavior of Peter after Jesus returns to His Father—martyrdom is merely the expected cost of a great love, as Jesus has already demonstrated. We're compelled to *do things* with and for the people we have a consuming love for; the fundamental pursuit of all great loves is to fully enter into the life of the Beloved.

My dream is exhibit A in the case for Tom Melton's dictum: "That which is most personal is most universal." Our deepest longings are all rooted in relationship, life, adventure, and a profound sense that our strength is needed. It might be melodramatic wish fulfillment, but on the other hand, God Himself is melodramatic (close your eyes and stab your finger pretty much anywhere in the Bible, and you'll prove my point). And, anyway, from where do our deepest wishes emanate?

It's not hard to see that the metaphoric core of my dream perfectly describes the spiritual and emotional reality of Peter's predicted future.

Jesus tells him that the cycle of his sifting will propel him into a grand and redemptive adventure, where his mission will be to "strengthen his brothers." When he is revealed after he is beaten and separated, Peter will have a new capacity to bring life-giving strength to the broken and grieving children of God. This is because he will, finally, be living out of his true name, pursuing his true mission as he acts on his true love for his Master. Jesus' assumption of coming strength in his sifted friend Peter is both a projection of certainty and an invitation—it's just another way of saying, "Enter into the joy of your master" (Matt. 25:21). And "the joy of our Master" is, again, Jesus' job description: "To set the burdened and battered free" (Luke 4:18 MSG).

What makes God happy—*intensely happy?* Well, when we abide in Him like a grafted-in branch, intimately and profoundly connected to Him and therefore involved in whatever He's doing. In Ephesians 1:11–12 Paul says, "It's in Christ that we find out who we are and what we are living for. Long before we first heard of Christ and got our hopes up, he had his eye on us, had designs on us for glorious living, part of the overall purpose he is working out in everything and everyone" (MSG). The more deeply we attach ourselves to Him, the more actively we join Him in His guerilla rescue force whose mission is to reach the burdened and battered, strengthening them and loving them in the midst of their own experiences of sifting. And as we offer our strength we discover who He has always meant us to be—our true name makes perfect sense to us.

Going into the Cave for Others

Back on the beach at the Sea of Tiberias, with the fresh smell of flame-broiled fish still in the air, Jesus drives home what "strengthen

your brothers" is going to look like for His friend the Rock. Imagine
for a moment you are Peter....

*You can still feel the warmth of the fire Jesus built
while you were cutting through the water to get to
Him. You've had a good breakfast and you can't stop
grinning because ... you're with Jesus again. He's flesh-
and-blood alive and, you now realize, staring right at
you—actually, His eyes are boring right through you.
He asks you to take a little walk with Him. You get up
and shake the sand off. Your soul is buzzing and you
can't stop glancing over at Him as you walk, unhurried
and aimless. Down the beach a little He finally turns,
flashes a half-smile, and asks a question that bites a
little: "Do you truly love Me more than any other?" A
little startled, you tell Him, "Yes, Lord; You know that
I love You." And in response, He simply says, "Feed My
lambs." Then you walk a little farther in silence. This
time He doesn't turn to you—His eyes are focused way
down the beach. There is no half-smile now. And He
asks again, "Do you truly love Me?" And you respond,
again, "Yes, Lord; You know that I love You." Now
He stops and turns—His face uncomfortably close to
yours—He won't take his eyes off you. "Take care of
My sheep," He says. Then, leaning further in, close
enough for you to feel His breath on your face, He asks
one more time, "Do you love Me?" And you can't hide
your hurt anymore. Tears well up in your eyes. You tell*

Him: "Lord, You know all things; You know that I
love You." And He backs away a little and studies your
anguished face—you see in His face both tenderness
and ferocity. And you see a grin just begin to creep
across His face as He says, one more time, with gravity,
"Feed My sheep." There's a long pause now as you walk
the beach in silence. You have the space to ponder what
it means to feed Jesus' sheep. You notice that Jesus has
quickened His pace and is now a few yards ahead of
you. And you rush to catch up as you see Him glance
back, throw back His head, and break into childlike
laughter.[1]

Here, "feed My sheep" is nonspecific, leaving plenty of room for
Peter to interpret and explore what it will mean for him. Whatever
expression he pursues, it will be unique to him because *he* is unique.
And, like Peter, we have to ponder what form "feed My sheep" will
take for us—this is the way we "work out [our] salvation" (Phil.
2:12). Each of us has something unique and beautiful to offer to
the "party of riders," but as with any adventure, there will be danger and risk and heartbreak and glory. And we will most often feel
awkward in the saddle. It's ironic that we treat "adventure" as such
a universally positive word when all true adventures will, at some
point, scare the poser out of us. We may pine for more adventure in
our lives, but when we're truly caught up in one, we are most often
desperate to get out of it. That's because we're not sure we really
have the *strength or courage* to live the adventure that's been shoved
down our throat.

Today we're in constant danger of being overwhelmed by all of the heartbreak and trouble that assault our senses from every corner of the world through print and screen. We are way, way too overexposed by the singular tortures of those whose babies have been strangled to death by faulty cribs, by wedding guests in Iraq blown up by a suicide bomber, by people drowned in their beachside homes during a tsunami, by seven-year-old girls sold into a lifetime of prostitution, and by high school students shot while they cower under their desks. It seems just too much for us to spread what little strength and empathy we have across such a vast sea of misery. Our ability to come alongside or even feel for so many who are bereft and destroyed is stretched to the breaking point. So we distance ourselves just to manage our capacity to care.

But God has set no such limits on His no-borders compassion. He sees and experiences everything—*every single heartbreak in every single heart.* He has journeyed up every mountain of doom and faced every horrible injustice. He never turns away from the unwatchable destructions that pervade the everyday life experiences of His seven billion children. While He is perpetually and infinitely heartbroken over our breaking and breaking and breaking, He's also perpetually and infinitely engaging us in our journey through the valley of the shadow of death. He will not turn from or abandon those who are right now going feetfirst through the wood chipper. He wants us to experience His presence viscerally, and so He has done something so unspeakably humble that it's hard for us to realize its true gravity. He has determined to reach His children in their darkness, to bring them the light of His presence, through the physical presence of His extended body—"The church is Christ's body, in which he speaks and acts" (Eph. 1:23 MSG). Who is doing the "speaking and acting" on behalf of Jesus? That would be you and me, His body.

God has chosen to *move with us and through us* in His mission of redemption (I don't like the word *use* that's so often thrown around in reference to God's movement in our lives—*use* is not how a father would describe the way he relates to his children). He could do it alone, but He chooses not to. He opts for attachment-relationship rather than application-edict. So, He's looking for men and women who will respond to His beckoning hand and, well, saddle up with Him, ready to ride into the darkest places on earth on behalf of His troubled and besieged children. And the people most likely to act on His invitation are those who are on the other side of their sifting—the beaten, separated, and revealed. He needs lovers who will risk it all for Him because they have already lost the husk of their false identities and are left only with the eternal kernels of their true selves. "Feed My sheep" is a forceful command—it's something we do that has a profound effect on the survival of the sheep. And the something we do is, simply, to offer our exposed and revealed "kernel of wheat" as sustenance for others, for the purpose of sifting is to reveal the only thing that is nourishing on the wheat stalk. With the husk fallen away under the force of the beating, the kernel—the life-giving essence—can now be offered as food for the hungry. Literally, when we are beaten, separated, and revealed we are able to "feed His sheep" because we have something nourishing to give. The "feed" we offer is not, as we assume, something *outside* of us—it *is* us. But it will mean we will have to move, not hang back. *You love Me? Good. My "love language" is simple—be willing to give to others what they need most.*

Those who learn to speak God's love language[2] are people who are much like the two men entrusted with five and two talents in the parable of the talents (Matt. 25:14–30)—people who live all-in for their Master by risking everything, in contrast to the one who fearfully buries the one talent entrusted to him because he knew the Master "to be a hard man, reaping where [he] did not sow and gathering where [he] scattered no seed" (v. 24). It's a fundamental misread of the Master's good heart—the third servant sees a scary tightwad instead of a shrewd Lover. People who've been sifted and revealed see God's heart more clearly, and therefore understand His goodness more deeply, and therefore give what they have to give more freely.

In Peter Jackson's film version of J. R. R. Tolkien's *The Return of the King*, the king-in-waiting Aragorn responds to the elven Lord Elrond's challenge—*"Put aside the Ranger—become who you were born to be"*—and heads off, alone, to travel the abandoned Dimholt road. At the end of that haunted path he will find the entrance to the mountain tomb of an army host of dead souls—disgraced warriors who will never be at rest until they have reversed their cowardly retreat from battle many centuries before. Aragorn intends to confront these apparitions and compel them to heal their shame by fighting with him and others who stand between the evil and the good. Fueled by his reclaimed identity and finally ready to give what he has to give, he tries to sneak out of camp without his friends by his side, but the elf Legolas and the dwarf Gimli are not fooled and insist on accompanying their friend into hell. When they arrive at the gates of the dead, their horses are so panicked that they bolt and run. The mouth of the cave smells like death. And Aragorn, turning to his friends, says, "I do not fear death!" and plunges into the darkness, soon followed by the elf and the dwarf.[3]

This scene, like my dream of the horsemen, is a compelling metaphor for the life Jesus has called us to—akin to His "mount up, son," it is "enter into the cave on behalf of others in need of rescue." Those of us who respond will have to stride into our own dark caves that smell like death, and the caves of others, plunging into the fearful unknown for the sake of their freedom and our own. Our role is to stand between the evil and the good when we are faced by insurmountable odds and hampered by our own weaknesses and wounds. When we do, we are simply responding to Jesus' passion:

> Jesus went through all the towns and villages, teaching in their synagogues, preaching the good news of the kingdom and healing every disease and sickness. When he saw the crowds, he had compassion on them, because they were harassed and helpless, like sheep without a shepherd. Then he said to his disciples, "The harvest is plentiful but the workers are few. Ask the Lord of the harvest, therefore, to send out workers into his harvest field." (Matt. 9:35–38 NIV)

It turns out, "the harvest is plentiful" means that we are surrounded and immersed and sometimes assaulted by the "harassed and helpless"—people who desperately need someone to "go into the cave" on their behalf. In my stumbling attempts to live this out through repeated cycles of sifting *(beaten, separated, and revealed)* I

have, of course, sometimes botched things terribly. But sometimes
I have offered the harassed and helpless a pathway to rescue, a hope
they'd all but given up on. I have many examples I *could* share,
but very few I *can* share—they're intimate and raw and weighted
with a kind of brokenness that demands confidentiality. Right now
my wife and I have been in the cave that smells like death for six
months on behalf of a close friend who was on her way to commit
suicide when she stopped by our house to give us her journals and
other personal papers—so that others would know her "true me"
after she was gone. And I have a friend who continues his regular
mission trips to Juarez, Mexico, with a small team of men who are
skilled at construction—on their own, they build homes for the
impoverished in the murder capital of the world. Not long ago a
man with connections to a drug cartel warned one of my friend's
"hosts" that the cartel had targeted these men for death. When I
asked my friend if he was going to continue his work, he flashed a
defiant look at me and said, "If the Christians leave, what hope will
anyone have?"

When we go into the cave, we often must contend with life and
death, and that can buckle our knees. God is asking us to go there
often ("send out workers into His harvest" [Matt. 9:38]) so that we
get over our panic and our fear and our cowardice and, as a result,
hold out our "kernel" of hope in the darkness—no matter what we
receive in return. In film and fiction, people who risk on behalf of
others' freedom are almost always rewarded somehow, but that artistic contrivance marks the dividing line between reality and creative
license. Yes, we're invited to join God in the glorious adventure of
His rescue mission. But I can say from personal experience, it's dark

in that cave—my wife and I have suffered injury many times over as we have ventured in. But going into the cave is not about what we will *get* from the experience; it's about what Jesus is asking us to *give*. This is why, in Luke 6, He asks us to do what seems impossible—to give to people who will *never* appreciate us for it:

> If you love those who love you, what credit is that to you? Even "sinners" love those who love them. And if you do good to those who are good to you, what credit is that to you? Even "sinners" do that. And if you lend to those from whom you expect repayment, what credit is that to you? Even "sinners" lend to "sinners," expecting to be repaid in full. But love your enemies, do good to them, and lend to them without expecting to get anything back. Then your reward will be great, and you will be sons of the Most High, because he is kind to the ungrateful and wicked. (vv. 32–35 NIV)

Jesus is telling us that "[children] of the Most High," later called the body of Christ by the apostle Paul, practice the unmistakable behavior patterns of God. The head and heart tell the hands and feet what to do—that's how a body works. And Jesus wants His hands and feet to get cave-dirty. Clearly, this is not the stuff of *Mister Rogers' Neighborhood*. People who say, "I do not fear death," are not merely nice, in the same way that Jesus is not merely nice. They go into dark places because that's where Jesus is, and they want to be always near Jesus.

The Courage We Need and the Courage We Don't

Of course, we'll need courage to enter into the dark caves of others with redemptive impact, but it's not the kind of courage we can "work up." The courage of the free is the fruit of our attachment to Jesus—its effect is epic but its practice is most often limited to what might be called the mundane moments of our lives. Grandiose courage intoxicates us. We turn the people who seem to have it into gods, but it's the everyday courage we *really* need. Murdered Columbine High School student Cassie Bernall quickly gained posthumous fame when another student who survived the massacre said he heard her answer yes when killer Dylan Klebold pointed his sawed-off shotgun at her and asked if she was a Christian. But in the months following the massacre, the girl who was hiding under a library desk near Cassie told police the exchange between Bernall and Klebold never happened. Instead, investigators later determined, the girl who answered yes to Klebold's question was most likely another girl, who actually survived the shooting— Valeen Schnurr.[4] So what difference does it make? Unfortunately, it makes *all* the difference to a hero-worshipping culture. Cassie's story of grandiose courage is so compelling that we can't give up our belief in it—much of the Christian world has held on to the Cassie-said-yes myth, even in the face of the facts. Why? I think we crave the stories of larger-than-life people who respond *just right* under the most extreme circumstances because, like my reverence for Shackleton's epic courage, we're longing to worship "safer gods." But true heroism is rarely grandiose—it works quietly to beat back the rock-eating termites in the lives of those who are burdened and battered.

It's telling, and sad, that a more meaningful story of Bernall's heroism is overshadowed by her supposed yes in the face of a killer. Long before that horrific day in April 1999, she'd made countless courageous, unnoticed, and uncelebrated decisions to defend her tender faith in Christ. In the book *She Said Yes,* Misty Bernall describes how her daughter, over and over, reaffirmed her faith by tiny heroisms. She'd been a hellion before her surprising conversion to Christ and had struggled to fit in to a Christian community she knew little about. Cassie's friend Cassandra recounts a conversation she had with her a few months before the Columbine rampage: "She said to me, 'You know, I don't even feel God anymore. God seems so far away. I'm going to keep pushing on, but it's really hard right now; I just don't feel Him anymore.'"[5] This is the courage we need to face down the rock-eating termites. And this is entering into the cave—into the dark unknown—because we're attached to Jesus like a grafted-in branch to the Vine. Grandiose courage is so seldom required of us that it hardly warrants our attention. But everyday courage, the hanging-on, pushing-on kind that's often never seen or acknowledged by others, is a precious treasure—because it's the kind of courage we have to have when the termites swarm.

Diamond is the little boy at the center of a coming-of-age story in George MacDonald's fantasy novel *At the Back of the North Wind.* In the midst of his poor and heartbreaking life, Diamond hears the voice of the North Wind (metaphorically, the Spirit of Christ) beckoning him to spend his "attachment" courage on behalf of his beleaguered family. After he takes his first tentative steps to obey, Diamond debriefs his experience with the North Wind:

"But I wasn't brave of myself," said Diamond, whom my older readers will have already discovered to be a true child in this, that he was given to metaphysics. "It was the wind that blew in my face that made me brave. Wasn't it now, North Wind?"

"Yes: I know that. You had to be taught what courage was. And you couldn't know what it was without feeling it: therefore it was given you. But don't you feel as if you would try to be brave yourself next time?"

"Yes, I do. But trying is not much."

"Yes, it is—a very great deal, for it is a beginning. And a beginning is the greatest thing of all. To try to be brave is to be brave. The coward who tries to be brave is before the man who is brave because he is made so, and never had to try."[6]

Jesus primes our "courage pump" by transfusing His own courage through our attachment to Him. When we first taste something of Him in ourselves, it gives us the impetus to start doling out what He's already given us. More deeply than any other desire, He wants to share what is His with us—He told His Father so on the eve of His crucifixion: "My prayer is not for them alone. I pray also for those who will believe in me through their message, that all of them may be one, Father, just as you are in me and I am in you. May they also be in us so that the world may believe that you have sent me" (John 17:20–21 NIV). Jesus wants for us to be *in Him*. And when we are *in Him*, we will share in His life. And we will carry His strength with us as we follow Him into all the dark alleys in the world, where His good heart longs to touch and heal and encourage the burdened and battered.

But why, when we know the by-product of our salvation is the gift of the Spirit of Christ, do we so often struggle to offer His strength? We are not *rhetorically* His body—this metaphor, like all God's metaphors, describes an actual truth about us. Our born-again reality is that we bring physical expression to God's desires in the world. Our physical body is responsible for living out the commands of our mind, will, and emotions—it simply does what it's told to do. That is, unless there's a blockage in the nervous system (such as multiple sclerosis or damage to the spinal cord) that hampers the body from doing what it's told to do. The beating our soul takes during life not only hampers our ability to act as the body of Christ, it thwarts us from receiving the help we most need.

Our good friends Brandon and Charity take in dogs that have been abandoned and brutalized. One of them is named Shorty, a shaking little wisp of a mongrel who looks like a pair of quivering eyes encased in a ball of black-and-white electrified hair. The first time I saw Shorty I said, "That dog looks like she was just kicked about five seconds ago." Her darting eyes are perpetually frightened and her body is always fibrillating. When she's fed, she waits until the other dogs have gobbled their food, and then, even though she's not threatened by anyone or anything, she dashes in to grab a little food from her dish and takes it under a table to eat it in "safety." She always eats this way. Shorty has been with them for two years, and she's only now starting not to flinch when Brandon makes a move toward her. She will be reacting out of her broken trust for the rest of her life—it will haunt all of her actions and interactions. *And she is more like us than we'd like to admit.* The world is full of "Shortys" who, because they have survived great wounds and endured terrible brutalities, are their own worst enemies. In their hurt they push away others who would love them. How will they ever open themselves to the healing they so desperately need? And, consequently, how will they ever offer their strength in service to the King if they are not healed and released into freedom?

One day, after a barbecue together, Bev saw Brandon cut up the leftover hamburgers—enough to feed their whole family again—and, instead of saving them for another meal, give the pieces to Shorty and her grateful sisters. It was a quietly extravagant thing to do. In that moment it dawned on us that Brandon and Charity are always doing things like this—patiently pursuing these broken and untrusting dogs the same way Jesus has asked His body to offer His relentless love to those who live in dark caves and feel bereft and alone ("to look after orphans and widows in their distress" [James 1:27 NIV]). The heart of Christ asks the body of Christ to give from its good treasure—offering not the cautious reciprocal love of a people who live in fear but the extravagant and strengthening love of a "rescue force" that is free to give.

Our Glorious Reduction

Diamond has the strength-offering capability of a child—something that, for a time, will come naturally to him. But he and I and you and everyone "grow out of" this sort of childlike response to the grace of God. At our church's vacation Bible school the leaders surprised the kids by suddenly dumping a host of beach balls on them from the balcony above. One little girl was laughing and delighted right up to the moment a beach ball that was ten times the size of her head bopped her. Startled, she rubbed her head a little, then spent the rest of the time with her hands above her head, coiled and ready to fend off the next assault. This is a perfect picture of the progressive effect of our wounding. The "arrows that fly by day"—the ones that find their mark in us as we wrestle through our days in enemy territory—make us wary and protective. We are cautious when little children are reckless, tense when they are delightfully goofy, calculating when they are obedient, suspicious when they are trusting, undermining of authority when they are grateful for it, stingy when they are ridiculously generous, stiff dancers when they are wild, and insecure when they are un-self-conscious.

Jesus tells the respected and influential Jewish Pharisee Nicodemus that he must be "born again" to see the kingdom of God—there is no other way to experience life the way the Trinity lives it. And the learned man responds just as we would—"Huh?" Or, more faithful to the text: "How can a man be born when he is old? He cannot enter a second time into his mother's womb and be born, can he?" (John 3:4).

Like so many others who respond to Jesus literally instead of metaphorically (I tell myself that's why my family seems oblivious to my obscure sense of humor most of the time), Nicodemus misses the point. And, it's true: Those who have never turned to Jesus during and after their sifting will always miss the point. As Jacques Ellul says, "It's only when we understand the Lordship of Jesus Christ that we are truly free."[7] Sifting alone has the power to reduce us to childlikeness, because it brutally wrests control from us and reminds us who is Lord. When control is a distant memory, only *then* do we understand the lordship of Jesus. The central deceit of Satan from the dawn of his betrayal is: *"You can be like gods—why live under obedience when you can demand it instead?"* Adam and Eve succumbed to this temptation, and "you can be like gods" is now ground zero for all our temptations. At the core of this deception is our hunger for control, and it's like a drug to us now. Detox from our addiction will require a sifting. On the other side of the beating and separating we endure is dependence and attachment—once an offense to us, these now seem not only possible but preferable responses to the grace of God. Soon they become our lifestyle.

Peter's emergence into childlike dependence will enable him to *strengthen his brothers* because he will be giving out of his attachment to Jesus, not out of his bravado. Yesterday he ran from an accusing child. Tomorrow he will stand up in the crowded temple court and tell everyone there—both the rulers and the rabble—that they crucified the King of Kings. If he wanted to commit suicide this would be a brilliant plan—jab your finger at the conniving power brokers who'd just managed to lynch Jesus. But he is not mobbed and torn to pieces; instead, "that day there were added about three thousand souls" (Acts 2:41). Now the Simon of yesterday is acting like the Peter of now and forever; he is living out of his true name, like a man born again. His childlikeness is dangerous—in the end, it will change the world.

Before he is crucified upside down at his own request, the fisher-of-men Peter will …

- stand in front of the most learned men of his day, "schooling" them in their theology and exposing their cowardice in the light of his courage. ("When they saw the courage of Peter and John and realized that they were unschooled, ordinary men, they were astonished and they took note that these men had been with Jesus" [Acts 4:13 NIV].)

- heal a man crippled from birth just by looking at him. ("Silver or gold I do not have, but what I have I give you. In the name of Jesus Christ of Nazareth, walk" [Acts 3:6 NIV].)

- refuse to stop speaking about the saving grace of Jesus, even under threat of violence. ("Judge for yourselves whether it is right in God's sight to obey you rather than God. For we cannot help speaking about what we have seen and heard" [Acts 4:19–20 NIV].)

- operate at such a fundamental level of faith that his mere presence radiates healing ("As a result, people brought the sick into the streets and laid them on beds and mats so that at least Peter's shadow might fall on some of them as he passed by" [Acts 5:15 NIV].)

- supernaturally escape from a locked and guarded prison cell, then endure a physical beating from the Sanhedrin's thugs with a promise of more to come if he didn't stop talking about Jesus ("The apostles left the Sanhedrin, rejoicing because they had been counted worthy of suffering disgrace for the Name" [Acts 5:41 NIV].)

I could go on and on, marching through the book of Acts, cataloging the outworking of Peter's strength flowing through the early body of Christ. Simon Peter's sifting has stripped his soul of his barnacle-identity—it has diminished the "Simon" and accentuated the "Peter." For him and for us, a false identity is the natural result of sailing our ships out of the safe harbor of childhood and into the rough waters of adult relationships and responsibilities. We are imprisoned by our crippling self-consciousness—all of us. Our wounds, like the abuse little Shorty endured during the early part of her life, make us cautious and calculating and self-centered. We all have MS of the soul.

A month ago, for my birthday, I told Bev I wanted only one birthday gift—to go to a downtown jazz club and hang out for an hour or two. So, along with our good friend Jill, we drove into Denver's nightclub district, parking a couple of blocks from the club. As we piled out of the car I was very aware of how odd it felt to be doing this—we are older parents of little kids, and our evenings are usually winding down at 9:00 p.m., not revving up. I had my arm around Bev while Jill walked next to us. Bev said, excitedly, "Rick, why don't you put each of us on an arm—you can stroll up to the club with your 'two ladies' on either side of you." And, I'm embarrassed to say, I was quickly gripped by self-consciousness.

"I'm not the kind of guy who struts, Bev."

"Oh come on, it'll be fun! And Jill is walking here all alone."

"No, I don't think so. I'd feel like a pimp—like Huggy Bear in that old *Starsky and Hutch* cop show."

And so we bantered this way all the way to the club—and I never offered my arm to Jill. Once inside the tiny place we saw that there were few places to sit. Only the booth directly in front of the stage was left, and that was because the musicians were stowing their gear in it. I asked the manager if we could sit there, and he cleared it for us. The show was about to start, and because I was literally inches away from the musicians I could see we weren't going to hear any jazz that night—it was a four-member blues band led by a scary-looking woman on electric guitar. The neck of the bass player's ax was literally sticking out in front of my face like a tree branch. The woman growled into the mic and the band kicked in to a raucous blues number that sounded like a jet taking off—the back of our booth was vibrating. I looked back at Bev and she had her fingers in her ears. I turned back to the band and realized I was smiling ear to ear—the funk and the noise and, most of all, the utter lack of distance between the music and me had transported and transformed me. I might as well have been onstage with them—the intimacy of the music had transcended my self-consciousness.

After an hour of this throbbing jubilation, Bev's ears were ringing and it was obvious we needed to go. We squeezed through the crowd and out the door. I looked at Bev and Jill, beaming, and then dramatically offered each of them an arm—we strutted all the way back to our car, just like Huggy Bear in *Starsky and Hutch*. One hour of really loud blues music, played very well, made me a child again, free and fully myself and able to give my strength when, before, my "adult sensibilities" had neutered me. For a few minutes I forgot my self-consciousness, in the same way my experiences of sifting have freed me from it. Sifting, apparently like loud blues music played inches from your ears, reveals our childlike true nature and clears the way for us to "give what we have to give"—and what we have to give is our strength. Children who are convinced their parents are strong, caring, and unconditionally *for* them spend very little time considering their fears. In contrast, we often act as if our good Father is untrustworthy and abusive, spending most of our lives warding off fears expressly because we're feeding at the pig's trough of our own insecure strength. Sifting blows away the clouds of self-dependence, revealing the bright and burning strength of our Father, who invites us to attach to Him and abide in Him so that we have something solid to give.

When Tom and Jill Melton's son Nick was a teenager he was caught and consumed by a drug-abusing lifestyle that they would later realize was brought on by the secret and abusive encounters he'd had with an adult as a little boy. In the middle of this heartbreak, when Tom was feeling the full impact of this sifting, he had an encounter with Satan on a lonely mountain road:

> We were on a retreat, and we almost always got a phone call about Nick getting into trouble when we were away from home. So, of course, we got one during that retreat. I went walking out on the road near the retreat center and had a conversation with Satan—it seemed like I was talking directly to him. I started cursing him. I said: "Bring it on, you ********. What else can you do to me?" It's like when I was playing center and middle guard for my high school football team, and we were getting our butts kicked by a much better team—it was something like sixty to nothing. By the fourth quarter

the coach had taken out all the starters, except for me. Inside, I was wishing he'd take me out, too. But then I thought, *What the heck—what else can they do to me?* After you've been beaten, and you know you have no chance of winning, you can just decide you're going to stay in the game and fight your heart out, no matter what happens. Bring it on!

Three of Nick's friends died that year—two from heroin overdoses and one from suicide. I was sitting in the living room with the parents of one boy who'd died of an overdose. I asked if they knew where the boys were getting the heroin from. The parents said they knew they were getting it from gangsters in the local Mafia, but they were afraid to rat them out because they might blow up their house. And I said: "They already killed your son! What do you have to lose?"[8]

Of course, the great singer/songwriter Kris Kristofferson acted the theologian when he parsed this truth in his song "Me and Bobby McGee": "Freedom's just another word for nothin' left to lose."[9] When we have been cut to our core—when we have been beaten, separated, and revealed—the constraints on our courage melt away. We have plenty to lose, but we don't live as if we have plenty to lose. Instead, we feel free to jab Satan in the eye, just as Tom did on that lonely mountain road. Spurgeon reminds us that the great reformer Martin Luther had, many times, done a little jabbing of his own: "Luther once threw an inkstand at [Satan's] head when he was tempting him very sorely, and though the act itself appears absurd enough, yet it was a true type of what that greater reformer was all his life long, for the books he wrote were truly a flinging of the inkstand at the head of the fiend. That is what we have to do: we are to resist him by all means. Let us do this bravely, and tell him to his teeth that we are not afraid of him."[10]

When we are freed from the illusion of control in our lives, we are also free to offer the generous and extravagant love of God to those who need it most. The great fourth-century mystic John Chrysostom said: "[The abundant grace] we have received was not a medicine only to [heal] the wound [of sin], but even health, and comeliness, and honor, and glory and dignities.... When all manifestly run together in one, there is not the least vestige of [death] left, nor can a shadow of it be seen, so entirely is it been done away."[11]

I grew up convinced that I was too much for everyone around me—a false belief that grew, more and more, because I suspected the people in my life were always striving to contain me. In the human mirrors that surrounded me I saw my reflection, and I looked a lot like a guy who was pretty hard to handle—of course, I'm solely responsible for embracing that reflection. But because I did embrace it, I believed that who I was at my core was too much for my parents, too much for my friends, and too much for God. Well into my fourth decade on earth, God's consistent response to this lie has been: "There is nothing, nothing, nothing too much for Me, including you. Bring it on! Attach to Me, and you will discover that nothing will be too much for *you*." Now that I am His, sharing in His life and "feasting on the fatted calf" as His reclaimed son, I've mounted up with Him many, many times. The fruit of sifting in my life is much the same as the fruit of sifting in Peter's life—it is, as

George MacDonald wrote in *Phantastes*, just this: "One wine is left in the broken bowl—'tis to love, and love, and love."

Like Peter, we are not overwhelmed or destroyed by our sifting because we are never alone in it. We have our Lord Jesus, who is fundamentally for us and fanatically hopeful about us. And we have a larger community of cheering fellow travelers—the sifted survivors who have been uniquely beaten and separated but universally revealed—men and women who have gone before us into the grand adventure, who smell like sweat and leather.

My seven-year-old daughter plays soccer, like every other seven-year-old girl in America, apparently. And after every game the parents create a human tunnel on the field by facing each other, grabbing our upraised hands, and forming an arch. The highlight of the day for these girls is running through that tunnel as all the parents cheer them on. I know it's the highlight because those girls come out one end of the tunnel and race to go back in on the other end. They'd do it all day if we had the patience to stand there.

I wish we could all be kids again and experience the unabashed for-ness of our "elders," going back through the tunnel over and over until we drop in happy exhaustion. This scene is a nearly perfect metaphor for what's happening in heaven right now—we know this is true because Hebrews 11 and 12 describes it for us. I don't know what our "cloud of witnesses" tunnel looks like, but I bet it's impressive and somehow really, really bright inside there. The revelation of the strength we have to give also gives us a glimpse and a taste of how much God enjoys us—how much He delights in our hidden labors, our endured sorrows, and our imperfect attempts to "give out of our good treasure."

We were made, and then redeemed, to glorify God—and the way God would like us to do that is by bringing "strength to our brothers." Nothing is more congruent with what is most true about us, and most true about the relentless heart of God. And yet, so often, the false self that has not yet been sifted cannot, and will not, give what the true self has to give. We need a severe mercy, and it is truly severe—because *beaten, separated, and revealed* is nothing if not unendurable. But we do endure. And the glory of God rises up from the pile of ashes around our feet, which is the incinerated shell that we have unwittingly passed off as our solid core. The outcome of Peter's journey through the sifter, and our own journey from "broken and broken and broken" to "strengthen your brothers," is perfectly summed up by Tonio K.:

> *You can't see your jailer*
> *You can't see the bars*
> *You can't turn your head round fast enough*
> *But it's everywhere you are*
> *It's all around you*
> *And everywhere you walk this prison yard surrounds you*
> *But in the midst of all this darkness*
> *In the middle of this night*
> *I see truth cut through this curtain like a laser*
> *Like a pure and holy light*
> *And I know I can't touch you now*
> *And I don't want to speak too soon*
> *But when we get sprung*
> *From out of our cages baby*
> *God knows what we might do*[12]

A BENEDICTION

"Be the Pig."

—Slogan on a T-shirt—given by the owners of one of America's
top-rated restaurants, The French Laundry in Napa Valley, to the
employee who's given it his or her all over the course of the year. It
refers to the difference between pigs and chickens—a chicken might
offer up an egg for the meal, but the pig gives his life for it.

I hadn't seen my good friend John for months—life has a way of vaulting you out of the orbit that keeps you close to the people you most care about. So we agreed to meet at a coffee shop. I knew next to nothing about the twists and turns his life must have taken over the months of our absence from each other's lives. I wondered if our friendship might have cooled—whether he'd been offended by my unavailability. We sat across from each other at a tiny round table. He leaned forward, grabbed my hand hard, and, with tears forming in his eyes, said, "Rick, I really missed you." It was not a quick grab—he held onto my hand as his welling tears tracked down his cheeks. I began to cry. I wondered if others in the coffee shop were uncomfortable with our intimacy—two guys holding hands and crying over their orange scones.

I know the source of my own tears. John reminded me that his friendship goes deep with me—that he's *for* me and will always be *for* me. My tired soul found a ledge to stand on that afternoon. But what was the source of his tears? *"Rick, I really missed you."* As I was driving home that day I remembered something John had shared with me several years ago. One day, after we'd been together, he'd come home and was telling his wife about our time. And she told him: "I really like it when you meet with Rick—you're more yourself when you come home."

And this is, in the end, what we have to give out of our sifted, broken hearts—a more unadulterated experience of who we are (the revealed kernel) and thus a clearer reflection of who Jesus is. And it's a remarkable and overgenerous thing that our own emerging freedom would spill over and splash onto others so profoundly that they, too, oodge their way a little closer to Jesus and a little closer to their soul's beautifully redeemed *center*. When our life's reality is "more of Him" it is not true that the counterbalance is "less of me"; the dependent relationship with Jesus that sifting produces leads to "more of Him" *and* "more of me" ("I can do everything through him who gives me strength" [Phil. 4:13 NIV]). The effect is that we become better mirrors and more nourishing fruit for the people around us, and that is the way we "strengthen our brothers." The fruit we offer is not the produce of striving—it's the produce of the Vine. This is why Jesus paired "loving God" with "loving others" as the two greatest commandments (Luke 10:27)—the two are not only mutually dependent, they are the common produce of *beat, separate, and reveal.*

So the strength we give is the strength we get from Jesus; and the scars from our grafts are a visceral reminder of His "beyond category" love for us and our own unconditional love for Him—a stripped-naked love that has taken seed and is poking up through the surface of our weathered and wounded souls. We must remember the greater context of our sifting, well embedded in the "legal complaint" outlined by Satan when he confronts God and demands permission to sift Job. Like a prosecuting attorney, he insinuates that Job would never love, serve, and obey God had He not blessed the man with family, health, and riches. Take away all that blessing, Satan accuses, and Job's love for God will grow cold. He's implying that Job—and all of God's children—love Him only because of what they get from Him. We do not, he asserts, offer God the intrinsic or "ruined" sort of love that Peter professes in response to Jesus' question: "Do you also want to leave?" (John 6:67 MSG). But when Job is stripped of everything that would tempt him to love God for His fringe benefits—when he is beaten and separated and on the verge of being revealed—he effectively dismantles the Enemy's argument by vowing: "Though He slay me, I will hope in Him" (Job 13:15). This, by definition, is unconditional love. In its very essence it is "the fruit of the Vine." And it is also the essence of Peter's successive responses to the resurrected Jesus as they walk the beach together: "Lord, You know all things; You know that I love You."

Only those who've been sifted like wheat, then have offered themselves as food for God's beloved, have the clarity to proclaim that, in truth, they love God unconditionally—the same strain of love that saved them in the first place. The same love that wells up in the Vine and courses into the branch-that-was-dying. And when the cost of loving Him turns out to be our very lives, the beaten, separated, and revealed discover yet another kindred intimacy with Peter—our only concern is to avoid any outward comparisons to our Beloved's death on the cross. Jesus must stand alone, because He alone is good.

"May the God of Abraham, Isaac and Jacob rattle your bones with His mighty roar, comfort you with His holy song, and break your heart with His deep, deep love."

—Andrew Peterson[1]

NOTES

Introduction

1. Caroline Alexander, *The Endurance* (New York: Alfred A. Knopf, 1998).

2. Apsley Cherry-Garrard, *The Worst Journey in the World* (Middlesex, UK: The Echo Library, 2007), 3.

3. Stephen Ambrose, *Undaunted Courage* (New York: Simon & Schuster, 1996).

4. Eugene H. Peterson, *A Long Obedience in the Same Direction* (Downers Grove, IL: InterVarsity Press, 2000), 88.

5. J. R. R. Tolkien, *The Two Towers* (New York: Ballantine Books, 1965), 186.

6. Max Lucado, *A Gentle Thunder* (Nashville: Thomas Nelson, 2009), 170–71.

7. Tonio K., "You Will Go Free," *Romeo Unchained* © 1986 Word Entertainment. Used with permission.

8. Peterson, *A Long Obedience in the Same Direction*, 26.

9. From a *Group Magazine* survey of ten thousand teenagers and adults at Group workcamps during the summer of 2000. Published in "The Cool Church," *Group Magazine,* May/June 2001.

10. Ira Glass, "This I Used to Believe," *This American Life* 378, National Public Radio, April 17, 2009, http://www.thisamericanlife.org/radio-archives/episode/378/this-i-used-to-believe.

11. Nicholas Wolterstorff, *Lament for a Son* (Grand Rapids, MI: Wm. B. Eerdmans Publishing Co., 1987), 68.

12. Tonio K., "You Will Go Free." Used with permission.

Just a Little Night Music

1. The Council of Nicaea in AD 325 was the early church's first attempt to codify the Scriptures into books, chapters, and verses.

2. Michael Mann, Christopher Crowe, James Fenimore Cooper, John Balderston, et al., *The Last of the Mohicans,* directed by Michael Mann (1992; Los Angeles: Twentieth Century Fox, 2001), DVD.

3. C. S. Lewis, *The Great Divorce* (New York: HarperOne, 2009), 28.

4. Charles H. Spurgeon, "The Sword of the Spirit" (sermon, Metropolitan Tabernacle, London, UK, April 19, 1891).

Chapter 1: "Simon, Simon ..."

1. The Fray, "You Found Me," *The Fray* © 2009 Epic.

2. Trent Reznor, "Hurt," *The Downward Spiral* © 1995 Nothing Records.

3. Kurt Kuenne, *Validation* (2007; Los Angeles: Theatre Junkies, 2001), short film, www.youtube.com/watch?v=Cbk980jV7Ao.

4. *The Furious Longing of God* is the title of a 2009 book by Brennan Manning (David C Cook), where he explores God's passion for His children.

5. Johnny Cash, "A Boy Named Sue," *Johnny Cash at San Quentin* © 2006 Sony.

6. J. R. R. Tolkien, Fran Walsh, Philippa Boyens, Peter Jackson, "Andúril—Flame of the West," *The Return of the King,* directed by Peter Jackson (2003; Los Angeles: New Line Home Video, 2004), DVD.

7. This pattern of preparation prior to a formal time of listening for God's voice— "Silence your own voice, then silence the voice of the Enemy"—is something Bob Krulish taught me to do many years ago.

8. Used with permission.

9. Walter Wangerin (keynote talk, Hutchmoot, Church of the Redeemer, Nashville, TN, August 8, 2010).

10. From Psalm 91:5–6 (NIV): "You will not fear the terror of night, nor the arrow that flies by day, nor the pestilence that stalks in the darkness, nor the plague that destroys at midday."

11. Steven Curtis Chapman, "Our God Is in Control," *Beauty Will Rise* © 2009 Sparrow Records.

Chapter 2: "Satan Has Asked …"

1. "Mavis Staples: Newport Folk Festival 2009," National Public Radio, http://www.npr.org/templates/story/story.php?storyId=111367884.

2. From John 10:10: "The thief comes only to steal and kill and destroy; I came that they may have life, and have it abundantly."

3. Charles H. Spurgeon, "Christ the Conqueror of Satan" (sermon, Metropolitan Tabernacle, London, UK, November 26, 1876).

4. Bob Krulish, email message. Used with permission.

5. Christopher Hitchens and Douglas Wilson, "A 'Collision' of Beliefs: Atheist versus Theologian," interview by Guy Raz, *All Things Considered,* National Public Radio, October 25, 2009, http://www.npr.org/templates/story/story.php?storyId=114115179.

6. To explore more six-word memoirs, go to Six-Word Memoirs, http://www.Smithmag.net/sixwords.

7. Sir Arthur Conan Doyle, "The Adventure of the Beryl Coronet," in *The Adventures of Sherlock Holmes* (New York: Harper & Brothers, 1892), 278.

8. Charles H. Spurgeon, "Satan Considering the Saints" (sermon, Metropolitan Tabernacle, London, UK, April 9, 1865).

9. Tom Melton, conversation with the author.

10. David Hay, conversation with the author.

11. Ibid.

12. Greg Stier, conversation with the author.

13. Peter Shaffer, *Amadeus,* directed by Milos Forman (1984; Burbank, CA: Warner Home Video, 1997), DVD.

14. Greg Stier, conversation with the author.

15. Tom Melton, conversation with the author.

16. Spurgeon, "Satan Considering the Saints."

17. Ibid.

18. Ibid.

19. From my personal notes taken during an informal two-hour lecture and question-and-answer time with Dallas Willard at the Downing House in Denver, Colorado, January 3, 2010.

20. Mark Galli, *Jesus Mean and Wild* (Grand Rapids, MI: Baker Books, 2006), 112.

21. David Macaulay, *The Way Things Work* (Boston: Houghton Mifflin Company, 1988), 22.

22. From 1 John 3:8: "The Son of God appeared for this purpose, to destroy the works of the devil."

23. Tom Melton, conversation with the author.

24. Ryan Adams, "Let Us Down Easy," *Cardinology* © 2008 Lost Highway Records.

25. William Paul Young, interview by Thom Schultz, February 2010. Schultz is the founder and president of Group Publishing, for LifeTree Café—an innovative outreach strategy for churches that want to reach people who have an aversion to church but enjoy a good conversation. For more information, go to www.lifetreecafe.com.

26. Philip Yancey, *The Jesus I Never Knew* (Grand Rapids, MI: Zondervan, 1995), 78.

27. Benedict Fitzgerald and Mel Gibson, *The Passion of the Christ*, directed by Mel Gibson (2004; Los Angeles: Twentieth Century Fox, 2004), DVD.

28. From Prime Minister Winston Churchill's famous "never give in" speech to students at Harrow School, October 29, 1941.

29. John Wesley, *Wesley's Journal*, 1909.

Chapter 3: "To Sift You Like Wheat …"

1. Bob Krulish, conversation with the author.

2. David Edelstein, "A 'Titans' Remake, Clashing with Everything in Sight," *All Things Considered,* National Public Radio, April 2, 2010, http://www.npr.org/templates/story/story.php?storyId=125451924.

3. Diana Krall, "Every Time We Say Good-bye," *Quiet Nights* © 2009 Verve Music Group.

4. The Mavens' Word of the Day, "Tribulation," *Words @ Random,* May 30, 2001, http://www.randomhouse.com/wotd/index.pperl?date=20010530.

5. From Genesis 50:20, where Joseph says to his brothers: "As for you, you meant evil against me, but God meant it for good in order to bring about this present result, to preserve many people alive."

6. From Romans 8:38–40: "For I am convinced that neither death, nor life, nor angels, nor principalities, nor things present, nor things to come, nor powers, nor height, nor depth, nor any other created thing, will be able to separate us from the love of God, which is in Christ Jesus our Lord."

7. George MacDonald, *Guild Court* (New York: Harper & Brothers, 1868), 128.

8. Robert Powers, "I Quit Carrying a Gun," This I Believe, March 5, 2010, http://thisibelieve.org/essay/16903/.

9. Steven Soderbergh and Matt Damon, "Damon and Soderbergh Team Up and Inform," interview by Terry Gross, *Fresh Air,* National Public Radio, September 16, 2009, http://www.npr.org/templates/story/story.php?storyId=112859307.

10. DaVarryl Williamson, interview by the author.

11. Ibid.

12. Ibid.

13. From my personal notes taken during an informal two-hour lecture and question-and-answer time with Dallas Willard at the Downing House in Denver, Colorado, January 3, 2010.

14. Sandy Spittka, email message, April 2, 2010. Used with permission.

15. LifeTree Café is an innovative outreach strategy for churches that want to reach people who have an aversion to church but enjoy a good conversation—for more information, go to www.lifetreecafe.com.

16. William Paul Young, interview by Thom Schultz, February 2010.

17. Ibid.

18. "Oprah Talks to Bono," by Oprah Winfrey, O, The Oprah Magazine, April 2004, http://www.oprah.com/omagazine/Oprahs-Interview-with-Bono-U2-and-AIDS-Activism/2.

19. The Normals, "Black Dress," Coming to Life © 2000 ForeFront. Used with permission.

20. Brennan Manning, The Ragamuffin Gospel (Sisters, OR: Multnomah, 1990), 26.

21. George MacDonald, David Elginbrod (Charleston, SC: BiblioBazaar, 2007), 50.

22. Dan Allender, The Wounded Heart: Hope for Adult Victims of Childhood Sexual Abuse (Colorado Springs: NavPress, 1990), 247.

Chapter 4: "But I Have Prayed for You, Simon ..."

1. "Conjunction (grammar)," Wikipedia, http://en.wikipedia.org/wiki/Grammatical_conjunction, accessed March 14, 2011.

2. From Isaiah 55:8: "'For my thoughts are not your thoughts, neither are your ways my ways,' declares the LORD" (NIV).

3. Benedict Fitzgerald and Mel Gibson, The Passion of the Christ, directed by Mel Gibson (Los Angeles: Twentieth Century Fox, 2004), DVD.

4. Christian Smith and Melinda Lundquist Denton, Soul Searching: The Religious and Spiritual Lives of American Teenagers (New York: Oxford University Press USA, 2005). The book and its sequel, Souls in Transition (2009), are based on The National Study of Youth and Religion led by Dr. Smith. I served on the Public Advisory Board for the study.

5. C. S. Lewis, *The Lion, the Witch and the Wardrobe* (New York: HarperCollins, 1950), 182.

6. C. S. Lewis, *The Voyage of the Dawn Treader* (New York: Macmillan, 1970), 88–91.

7. From 1 Corinthians 13:7: "[Love] bears all things, believes all things, hopes all things, endures all things."

8. From 1 Corinthians 13:8: "Love never fails."

9. From Psalm 23:4: "Even though I walk through the valley of the shadow of death, I fear no evil, for You are with me; Your rod and Your staff, they comfort me."

10. Joseph Stein, *Fiddler on the Roof,* directed by Norman Jewison (1971; Los Angeles: MGM, 2007), DVD. It's based on the Broadway musical with music by Jerry Bock, lyrics by Sheldon Harnick, and book by Joseph Stein.

11. Jacques Ellul, *Perspectives on Our Age* (Toronto, ON: House of Anansi Press, 1997), 6.

12. Ibid.

13. Ibid., 7.

14. Andrew Niccol, *The Truman Show,* directed by Peter Weir (1998; Los Angeles: Paramount, 1999), DVD.

15. Charlie Hall, "Marvelous Light," *Flying into Daybreak* © 2006 Six Step Records.

Chapter 5: "That Your Faith May Not Fail ..."

1. "Ninja Myths," *Mythbusters,* 2007 season, episode 78, aired April 25, 2007.

2. Charles Schultz, *It's the Great Pumpkin, Charlie Brown,* directed by Bill Melendez (1966; New York: CBS, 2000), DVD.

3. From Acts 8:20: "May your silver perish with you, because you thought you could obtain the gift of God with money!"

4. Chad Arnold, "Faith Fracas," *Come Too Far,* October 23, 2010, http://come-toofar.com/?p=248. Used with permission.

5. Christopher Hitchens and Douglas Wilson, "A 'Collision' of Beliefs: Atheist versus Theologian," interview by Guy Raz, *All Things Considered*, National Public Radio, October 25, 2009, http://www.npr.org/templates/story/story.php?storyId=114115179.

6. Bruce Cockburn, "Pacing the Cage," *The Charity of Night* © 1997 Rykodisc.

7. Martin Luther King Jr. was a U.S. black civil rights leader and a Baptist clergyman (1929–1968).

8. Michael D. Warden, "Who You Really Are = What You Do Under Pressure, *The Sojourner Blog*, April 8, 2010, http://michaelwarden.com/blog/who-you-are-what-you-do-under-pressure. Used with permission.

Chapter 6: "And When You Have Turned Back …"

1. Avi Steinberg, "'Running the Books' in a Prison Library," interview by Neal Conan, *Talk of the Nation*, National Public Radio, October 19, 2010, http://m.gpb.npr.org/news/Books/130675521?singlePage=true.

2. "Liminal space" is a psychological term that means "a place where boundaries dissolve a little and we stand there, on the threshold, getting ourselves ready to move across the limits of what we were into what we are to be" ("Liminal space," http://parole.aporee.org/work/hier.php3?spec_id=19650&words_id=900).

3. Ron Block, "The Holy Baby," RonBlock.com, December 25, 2010, http://ronblock.com/2010/12/25/the-holy-baby. Used with permission.

4. Used with permission.

5. Steven Curtis Chapman, "Beauty Will Rise," *Beauty Will Rise* © 2009 Sparrow Records.

6. To watch a powerful and short treatise by Wintley Phipps (president of the U.S. Dream Academy, an organization that reaches out to the children of prisoners) on "Amazing Grace," go to http://www.youtube.com/watch?v=DMF_24cQqT0.

7. Steve Fitzhugh, "When Crisis Strikes," *Network Magazine*, Fall 2004.

8. Tom Waits, "San Diego Serenade," *The Heart of Saturday Night* © 1974 Elektra/ Asylum Records.

9. N. T. Wright, *Following Jesus* (Grand Rapids, MI: Eerdmans, 1994), ix.

10. Matt Damon and Ben Affleck, *Good Will Hunting,* directed by Gus Von Sant (1997; Los Angeles: Walt Disney Video, 1999), DVD.

11. Charles H. Spurgeon, "Peter's Restoration" (sermon, Metropolitan Tabernacle, London, UK, July 22, 1888).

12. Peter Kreeft, "The Shocking Beauty of Jesus" (lecture, Gordon-Conwell Seminary, South Hamilton, MA, September 20, 2007). He later expanded upon this topic in his book *Jesus-Shock.*

Chapter 7: "Strengthen Your Brothers."

1. This is a retelling of the postresurrection beachside scene with Jesus and some of His disciples in John 21.

2. The concept of "love languages" was made popular by Gary Chapman in *The Five Love Languages* (Chicago: Northfield Publishing, 2010).

3. J. R. R. Tolkien, Fran Walsh, Philippa Boyens, Peter Jackson, "Dwimorberg— The Haunted Mountain," *The Return of the King,* directed by Peter Jackson (2003; Los Angeles: New Line Home Video, 2004), DVD.

4. Dave Cullen, *Columbine* (New York: Twelve, 2010), 226–30.

5. Misty Bernall, *She Said Yes: The Unlikely Martyrdom of Cassie Bernall* (Rifton, NY: Plough Publishing House, 1999), 86.

6. George MacDonald, *At the Back of the North Wind* (Middlesex, UK: The Echo Library, 2006), 71.

7. Jacques Ellul, *Perspectives on Our Age* (Toronto, ON: House of Anansi Press, 1997), 6.

8. Tom Melton, conversation with the author. Used with permission.

9. Kris Kristofferson and Fred Foster, "Me and Bobby McGee," *Kristofferson* © 1970 Monument.

10. Charles H. Spurgeon, "Christ the Conqueror of Satan" (sermon, Metropolitan Tabernacle, London, UK, November 26, 1876).

11. St. John Chrysostom, *Homilies on Romans,* OrthodoxEbooks, http://www. orthodoxebooks.org/sites/default/files/pdfs/Romans%20-%20Saint%20John%20 Chrysostom.pdf.

12. Tonio K., "You Will Go Free," *Romeo Unchained* © 1986 Word Entertainment. Used with permission.

A Benediction

1. Andrew Peterson, "The Christmas Tour 2005 Review," AndrewPeterson.com, December 19, 2005, http://www.andrew-peterson.com/forum/viewtopic.php?t=57 94&sid=f4930215b9d56aea2ec06ee9286a6162.